### *Impressed by Don's Gentle Spirit*

I met Don Gossett and his family at the *Southern Gospel Quartet Convention* in Nashville, in September 1972. I was impressed by Don's gentle and easy spirit; nothing forced, but he had an authority about him I hadn't seen before. I only got saved in 1971 and was still unsure of who I was in Christ. In the next 5 to 10 years, Don always reached out to encourage me to become conversant with the *"new creature"* I'd become. I wish there had been more time to be around him. My friend Judy Gossett (his daughter) would relate stories about growing up and traveling around the world with her father. He was always full of the Holy Spirit, Who was maneuvering you and protecting you through Don. An amazing man!

~ **Fletch Wiley**, World-class Musician, President of *Visual Music Productions*; Austin, Texas

### *His Was A Life Well Lived*

I am so, so sorry, my friend, to hear of your father's passing. His was a life well lived. The hole will be great; however the future is greater. I was honored to know him. I would not be who I am today without him.

~ **Tim Gilman**, Co-Founder and Creative Director, *Bethlehem Coffee Company*; Salem, Oregon

### *One of Our Favorite People*

I feel so honored to have met a man so incredibly great. He touched so many lives, and will be greatly missed! He was one of our favorite people.

~ **Kendi Lehman;** Albuquerque, New Mexico

### *An Inspiring Teacher and Leader*

He not only leaves his family but the multitudes of people he brought to the Lord! He was an inspiring teacher and leader. Try to take comfort knowing God has a special place for him in Heaven.

~ **Amber McPhail;** *Birch Bay, Washington*

### *He Fought the Good Fight, Kept the Faith*

So sorry for your loss but it is Heaven's gain. He fought the good fight and he kept the faith. He is experiencing unimaginable splendors in Heaven, and He wouldn't come back if he could. He will wait for you; I am looking forward to it myself.

~ **Terry Blackwood;** Contemporary Christian Music Singer; Nashville, Tennessee

### *Millions Of Lives Touched By His Faithfulness*

Brother Don will be encouraged to now see the millions of lives his faithfulness has touched. To this end, God shall wipe away his tears. I can hear through the Courts of Heaven: *"Well done!"*

~ **Bill Cahlendar;** *Saint Agnes Baking Company;* Minneapolis, Minnesota

### *Don's Written Words Gave Life*

I rejoice with you. Don's written words gave life and encouragement to me on many occasions. He will be missed.

~ **Cliff Tadema,** Senior Pastor; *Skagit Valley Christ the King Community Church;* Mount Vernon, Washington

## My NEVER AGAIN List
### By Don Gossett
#### A Bold Challenge to "Speak the Word Only"

*"The centurion answered and said, 'Lord, I am not worthy that Thou shouldest come under my roof; but speak the word only, and my servant shall be healed."* (Matthew 8:8)

FIRST: NEVER AGAIN will I confess **"I can't,"** for *"I can do all things through Christ which strengtheneth me"* (Philippians 4:13).

SECOND: NEVER AGAIN will I confess **lack**, for *"My God shall supply all my need according to His riches in glory by Christ Jesus"* (Philippians 4:19).

THIRD: NEVER AGAIN will I confess **fear**, for *"God hath not given me the spirit of fear, but of power, and of love, and of a sound mind"* (II Timothy 1:7).

FOURTH: NEVER AGAIN will I confess **doubt and lack of faith**, for *"God hath given to every man the measure of faith"* (Romans 12:3).

FIFTH: NEVER AGAIN will I confess **weakness**, for *"The Lord is the strength of my life"* (Psalm 7:1) and *"The people that know their God shall be strong and do exploits"* (Daniel 11:32).

SIXTH: NEVER AGAIN will I confess **supremacy of Satan over my life**, for *"Greater is He that is within me than he that is in the world"* (I John 4:4).

SEVENTH: NEVER AGAIN will I confess **defeat**, for *"God always causeth me to triumph in Christ Jesus"* (II Corinthians 2:14).

EIGHTH: NEVER AGAIN will I confess **lack of wisdom**, for *"Christ Jesus is made unto me wisdom from God"* (I Corinthians 1:30).

NINTH: NEVER AGAIN will I confess **sickness**, for *"With His stripes, I am healed"* (Isaiah 53:5) and *"Jesus Himself took my infirmities and bare my sicknesses"* (Matthew 8:17).

TENTH: NEVER AGAIN will I confess **worries and frustrations**, for I am *"Casting all my cares upon Him Who careth for Me"* (I Peter 5:7). In Christ, I am "care-free"!

ELEVENTH: NEVER AGAIN will I confess **bondage**, for *"Where the Spirit of the Lord is, there is liberty"* (II Corinthians 3:17). My body is the temple of the Holy Spirit!

TWELFTH: NEVER AGAIN will I confess **condemnation**, for *"There is therefore now no condemnation to them which are in Christ Jesus"* (Romans 8:1). I am in Christ – therefore I am free from condemnation!

(Copyright © 1961 by Don E. Gossett; all rights reserved; used with permission.)

# The Story Behind Don Gossett's *MY NEVER AGAIN LIST*

### By Jeanne Gossett Halsey

# The Story Behind Don Gossett's
# MY NEVER AGAIN LIST

By **Jeanne Gossett Halsey**

**ISBN  978-1-312-80456-2**

***The Story Behind Don Gossett's MY NEVER AGAIN LIST*** by Jeanne Michele Gossett Halsey (1953-); copyright © 2015; published by *ReJoyce Books*, a division of *Masterpieces In Progress Publishing House*; all rights reserved; ISBN 978-1-312-80456-2.  This book is protected under the Copyright Laws of the United States of America; all rights reserved under International Copyright Law.  No part of this book may be reproduced or transmitted in any form or by any means, electronic or mechanical, including photocopying, recording, or by information storage and retrieval system, in any manner whatsoever, without express written permission of the Author, except in the case of brief quotations embodied in critical articles and reviews.

Scriptures quoted from *The Holy Bible, King James Version* (KJV); Public Domain.  Scriptures quoted from *The Holy Bible, New Living*

*Translation* (NLT); copyright © 1996, 2004, 2007, 2013 by *Tyndale House Foundation*; used by permission of *Tyndale House Publishers, Inc.*; Carol Stream, Illinois, 60188; all rights reserved; used with permission. Scriptures quoted from *The Holy Bible, New International Version* (NIV); copyright © 1973, 1978, 1984, 2011 by *Biblica, Inc.*; all rights reserved worldwide; used by permission. Scriptures quoted from *The Message Bible* (MSG); copyright © 1993, 1994, 1995, 1996, 2000, 2001, 2002 by Eugene H. Peterson; all rights reserved; used with permission. Scriptures quoted from *The Holy Bible, Amplified Version* (AMP); copyright © 1954, 1958, 1962, 1964, 1965, 1987 by *The Lockman Foundation*; all rights reserved; used by permission.

*"Joy Unspeakable,"* by Barney E. Warren, 1900; Public Domain. *"What You Say Is What You Get,"* words and music by Reba Rambo and Dony McGuire; © 1977; published by *Designer Music/SESAC*; all rights reserved; used with permission. *"Never Again,"* words and music by Reba Rambo and Dony McGuire; arranged by Judy A. Gossett; © 1979; published by *Bud John Songs, Inc./ASACP and Oohs And Aahs Music/ASCAP*; all rights reserved; used with permission.

Unless otherwise noted, all photographs are from the Gossett Family Archives and the Halsey Family Archives; all rights reserved; used by permission.

Printed in the United States of America by Lulu.com.
For more information, contact:

*Masterpieces In Progress Publishing House*
4424 Castlerock Drive
Blaine, Washington  98230
United States of America

eMail:  halseywrite@comcast.net

# TABLE OF CONTENTS

Foreword by Rev. John W. Lucas, Jr. ................. 13
Introduction ....................................................... 15

## Part One: HIS STORY
## By Don Gossett

The Original *My Never Again List* ..................... 23
Don Gossett's Testimony .................................... 27

## Part Two: HOW IT HAPPENED
## By Jeanne Gossett Halsey

Chapter One: Agreeing With the Word ........... 37
Chapter Two: Learning Boldness ...................... 49
Chapter Three: Holy Heartburn ........................ 59
Chapter Four: Born to Conquer ........................ 69
Chapter Five: The Biggest Enemy ..................... 79
Chapter Six: Unlocking Chains .......................... 87
Epilogue: *Bold Bible Living* ............................. 97

## Part Three: TESTIMONIALS AND TRIBUTES

By Various Authors ........................................... 105

## Afterwords

Eulogy ............................................................... 153
Obituary ............................................................ 169

Dedication .................................................... 173
About the Author ............................................ 175
Other Titles ..................................................... 179
Postscript: My Father's Smile ......................... 191

# FOREWORD
By **Dr. John W. Lucas, Jr.**

Dr. Lucas speaking at the Memorial Celebration of the Life of Don Gossett. (January 10, 2015)

Soon after his move to Canada, I met Don Gossett and entered what became a life-long faith adventure. He referred to it as a "true friendship." We preached conventions, crusades and radio services together. I had the wonderful privilege of opening churches in several countries to his unique ministry, which grew to 60 nations.

When he heard I was going to speak at a Minister's Institute in East Africa, he immediately sent a large box of *MY NEVER AGAIN LIST* and five other *Bold Living* cards. They were to be the sermon emphasis each different day of the week-long event that was to be attended by 1,500 pastors and native missionaries. Don was a giver – liberally investing in the ministries of everyone he met.

His favorite crusade song was:

*"Thank You, thank You, Jesus*
*Thank You, thank You, Jesus, in my heart*
*You can't make me doubt it*
*I know too much about it*

*Thank You, thank You, Jesus, in my heart."*

In every service, he led that song with enthusiastic fervor, gently clapping his hands.

The revolutionary and simply-stated Biblical message proclaimed in MY NEVER AGAIN LIST has positively affected the lives of thousands around the world. *"Many rise up and called him blessed"* (see Proverbs 31:28) for Dr. Don Gossett's obedience to God's call upon his life, and using his anointed pen to effectively inform that there is a "better way" to overcome defeat, discouragement and depression. Read MY NEVER AGAIN LIST!

**Dr. John W. Lucas, Jr.**
Pastor Emeritus, *Immanuel Assembly of God;*
Retired National Coordinator, *The Fellowship of Christian Assemblies of Canada;*
Calgary, Alberta

# INTRODUCTION

In 2010, I sat down with my father Don Gossett and presented my idea of collaborating on writing a portion of his life story by keying it around one of his most life-changing and most-popular Christian teachings: **"MY NEVER AGAIN LIST."** I wanted us to tell of how God led him through very real, personal trials of his own into a greater understanding of the Bible, and how he learned to overcome difficult circumstances by applying God's written promises.

One reason for the book was *because I was there*, and I clearly remember the "before" and "after" changes in our family as we accepted and applied of the realities of *MY NEVER AGAIN LIST* (*MNAL*). As an 8-year-old girl in 1961, I literally watched the Word of God come alive in my parents' lives, and then personally experienced the impact of those changes in the way we thought, prayed, behaved, and lived. We five Gossett children *learned* these twelve principles for living; we even learned them in French: *"Je ne dirai jamais plus ..."*

In the 50-plus years since my father wrote those twelve original affirmations on the flyleaf of his Bible – and with the millions of copies distributed around the world – I witnessed Dad preach this sermon hundreds of times. A preacher's kid can become fairly jaded, but this sermon was always one of my favorites: intently I would scan the faces of the people in his audience and literally observe the truths of God's Word penetrating into their hearts, watch their expressions turn from doubt-full to faith-full, then hear their testimonies of changed lives as they too applied *MNAL* to their own lives. I was proud of my Daddy!

There were also the plagiarists. So many other ministries — savory and otherwise — "borrowed" *MNAL* and redistributed it as their own. It's not that any one man has a direct claim on God's Word and its application, but my father lived these problems (those "never again" things like "fear of man" and "lack of faith") himself, and these *MNAL* answers which God gave him through Scripture represented a man overcoming personal difficulties and walking as a new creature in Christ (see 2 Corinthians 5:17) for all of his life. Others copied him directly and took illicit credit for it; some eventually acknowledged the original source and made reparation. As his young daughter, I was highly offended that anyone would "steal from" my father; as his mature daughter, I still defend him, proud of the writing skill Dad had (and which is my primary inheritance from him today).

During that conversation in 2010, my father was excited about publishing the background story of *MNAL*, partly because he has always been an accomplished story-teller. In addition to reading Bible stories to we five children and feeding our imaginations with the long-play vinyl recordings of great story-tellers like Ethel Barrett, making up creative bed-time stories was one of Dad's fortés (a habit he carried into the next generation with his grandchildren). [*"The Becky Stories"* should have been written down and shared as important children's literature! "Becky" was a little girl who had such amazing adventures, and she always managed to include a time of prayer to her loving Heavenly Father as she successfully navigated another difficulty – what a great way to ingrain life-lessons to children!]

But when it came to writing his life-story, Dad hesitated. Even with zeroing in on his true life experience in 1961, my father was modest; he really didn't want to draw attention to himself but always point people to Jesus. This is possibly why he also steered away from allowing anyone to publish his actual biography (although that too has been in the works for years). So this book was shelved for four years; I promised him I would not publish it until after his death.

When I sat down in December 2014 to write the Eulogy for my father's Memorial, this then-75%-completed manuscript was tapping on my shoulder. I maintain that the central turning-point of my father's life was when his intense study of the Bible – and the direct application to the problem areas of his own life – brought about an enormous change, and a soaring faith that characterized the remainder of his 85-plus years.

This book – like the books I wrote and published to honor my mother Joyce Gossett (1929-1991), *Stubborn Faith: Celebrating Joyce Gossett*" and my sister Judy Gossett (1952-2003), *"Judy Becomes A Bride"* – is my tribute to my beloved father Don Gossett. This is only a part of his life-story, but it tells you a great deal about what shaped his life and ministry.

As I wrote the finishing touches to this book, I could hear the delightful song which long-time family friend Reba *"Other Sister"* Rambo-McGuire wrote (and which Judy masterfully arranged) about *MNAL:* simply titled *"Never Again,"* the theme rings clearly:

> *"I won't let my words defeat me*
> *I won't let my words defeat me*
> *I won't let my words defeat me*
> *Never again!"*

My prayer is that the living Word of God will sing in your heart as you read my father's story.

*I can do all things through Christ Who strengthens me!*
**Philippians 4:13**; NKJV

*Jeanne Michele* (née *Gossett*) *Halsey*
Birch Bay, Washington
March 2015

The 2012 cover photo (shown here) is one of my favorite portraits of my father, Don Gossett. It was taken at Radio KARI, where Dad was recording his daily 15-minute program of *Bold Bible Living*. The sheer joy of ministry that is depicted on his smiling face tells it all!

**Part One:
HIS STORY
By Don Gossett**

# MY NEVER AGAIN LIST
## By Don Gossett

**A Bold Challenge to *"Speak the Word Only"***

*The centurion answered and said, "Lord, I am not worthy that Thou shouldest come under my roof; but speak the word only, and my servant shall be healed."*
**Matthew 8:8; KJV**

1st: **Never Again will I confess "I can't,"** for *"I can do all things through Christ which strengtheneth me"* (Philippians 4:13; KJV).

2nd: **Never Again will I confess lack,** for *"My God shall supply all my need according to His riches in glory by Christ Jesus"* (Philippians 4:19; KJV).

3rd: **Never Again will I confess fear,** for *"God hath not given me the spirit of fear; but of power; and of love, and of a sound mind"* (II Timothy 1:7; KJV).

4th: **Never Again will I confess doubt and lack of faith,** for *"God hath given to every man the measure of faith"* (Romans 12:3; KJV).

5th: **Never Again will I confess weakness,** for *"The LORD is the strength of my life"* (Psalm 7:1; KJV) and "*The people that know their God* *shall be strong and do exploits"* (Daniel 11:32; KJV).

6th: **Never Again will I confess supremacy of Satan over my life,** for *"Greater is He that is within me than he that is in the world"* (I John 4:4; KJV).

7th: **Never Again will I confess defeat,** for *"God always causeth me to triumph in Christ Jesus"* (II Corinthians 2:14; KJV).

8th: **Never Again will I confess lack of wisdom,** for *"Christ Jesus is made unto me wisdom from God"* (I Corinthians 1:30; KJV).

9th: **Never Again will I confess sickness,** for *"With His stripes, I am healed"* (Isaiah 53:5; KJV) and *"Jesus Himself took my infirmities and bare my sicknesses"* (Matthew 8:17; KJV).

10th: **Never Again will I confess worries and frustrations,** for I am *"Casting all my cares upon Him Who careth for Me"* (I Peter 5:7; KJV). In Christ, I am "care-free"!

11th: **Never Again will I confess bondage,** for *"Where the Spirit of the Lord is, there is liberty"* (II Corinthians 3:17; KVJ). My body is the temple of the Holy Spirit!

> 12th: **Never Again will I confess condemnation,** for *"There is therefore now no condemnation to them which are in Christ Jesus"* (Romans 8:1; KJV). I am in Christ therefore I am free from condemnation!
>
> [Copyright © 1961 by Don E. Gossett; all rights reserved; used with permission.]

[AUTHOR'S NOTE: In 1967, Don Gossett added another eleven affirmations to create an expanded version of *MNAL*, but these are the original twelve written and published in 1961.]

## Chapter One: **My Testimony**
### By **Don Gossett**
*Reprinted with permission*

When the Lord led me to create *MY NEVER AGAIN LIST,* this truth literally changed my life. Quite often the phrase, *"This will change your life!"* is so bandied around carelessly and frivolously that it has become a diluted cliché, losing much of its power and veracity. But when I tell you that God literally changed my life with the truths contained in *MY NEVER AGAIN LIST,* it is an absolute fact.

Until that life-changing visitation of the Lord, I was continually defeated, trounced and routed. I was snared in the trap of my own negative words. I was constantly talking about my defeats and failures ... and I got exactly what I said: more defeats, more failures, more loss of self-esteem. Here is how God transformed my life.

In 1961, our family of seven had immigrated to Canada, where my wife Joyce and I felt God had called us to go. Our ministry there was sporadic, and frankly, we were floundering. We had settled our family into a small motel on Vancouver Island, in the city of Victoria, British Columbia. The little motel was close enough to a local school for our children to walk. I was traveling in evangelistic ministry all over Vancouver Island, some engagements on the mainland, some engagements up and down the Pacific coast states of Washington and Oregon.  Joyce would remain at the motel with the children, solo-parenting most of the time, while I went from church to church, preaching, and endeavoring to support the family.  We were poor, we were always broke, we were struggling.

One day, after being away from my family for several days, I was driving back to them ... and I was wallowing in negative, morbid thoughts.  I was dejected, disappointed and frustrated over the constant failures and losses in my life and ministry.  My personal and family needs were staggering.

Suddenly, the Spirit of the Lord arrested me, began to convict me of the "death words" – not the "life words" – that I had been thinking and speaking.  Aware this was an important moment with God, I quieted my heart and began to listen.

He began with this crucial verse:  *"How can two walk together unless they be agreed?"* (Amos 3:3).  He said, *"Don, how can you and I walk together  be traveling the same path, be reaching for the same goals, unless we are in agreement? How can you and I be partners in your life unless we are saying the same thing, believing the same thing, functioning in the same anointing?  Don't you know that I AM 'the Way, the Truth and the Life'?* (John 14:6) *I am **not** 'lost, unclear, death'!"*

With these challenging words resounding in my soul, I began to learn to agree with my loving, compassionate, empowering God and the truths He has so clearly written in His Word ... and to disagree with the wicked, vicious, hateful devil who had been wreaking such havoc in my life. Over and over, Bible verses began to crop up in my mind, reminding me of God's provision and direction for every problem I was facing. God challenged my perception of my own self, pointing out some of my personality flaws but also offering His answer to correcting those problems and *aligning myself with His personality and heart.* He visited my spirit with so many truths that I knew I had to write them all down ... and then was born *MY NEVER AGAIN LIST.*

The twelve original principles of *MY NEVER AGAIN LIST* dramatically and permanently changed my whole life, my family, my ministry, my finances, and my destiny! Salvation received at age 12 ... called to preach at age 17 ... baptism of the Holy Spirit at age 19 – each were precious, life-changing experiences for me ... but no experience since has rivaled the extraordinary impact of *MY NEVER AGAIN LIST.* This was a major turning point!

Jesus declared, *"You are My disciples"* (John 8:31, 14:15). A disciple is one who disciplines himself to follow. As I learned to daily affirm *MY NEVER AGAIN LIST,* **it became not only a discipline but also a "grade card" for my daily walk with the Lord** [emphasis added].

## "Speak the Word Only"

The subtitle to MY NEVER AGAIN LIST is *"Speak the Word Only."* This comes from the story in Matthew 8:

*When Jesus was entered into Capernaum, there came unto Him a centurion, beseeching Him and saying, "Lord, my servant lieth at home sick of the palsy, grievously tormented."*

*And Jesus saith to him, "I will come and heal him."*

*The centurion answered and said, "Lord, I am not worthy that Thou shouldest come under my roof. But **speak the word only,** and my servant shall be healed. For I am a man under authority, having soldiers under me; and I say to this man, 'Go,' and he goeth; and to another, 'Come,' and he cometh; and to my servant, 'Do this,' and he doeth it."*

*When Jesus heard it, He marveled, and said to them that followed, "Verily I say to you, I have not found so great faith; no, not in Israel!*

*"And I say to you that many will come from east and west, and sit down with Abraham, Isaac and Jacob in the Kingdom of Heaven. But the children of the Kingdom shall be cast*

*out into outer darkness; there shall be weeping and gnashing of teeth."*

*And Jesus said unto the centurion, "Go thy way; and as thou hast believed, so it be done unto thee." And his servant was healed in the selfsame hour.*
           **Matthew 8:5-13** (KJV); emphasis added

Jesus was born a Jew, and His ministry began to Jewish people. In that culture, Jews did not mingle socially or conduct business with Romans; it was a religious no-no. Yet somehow this Roman centurion had heard of Jesus, perhaps had listened from afar to His teachings, but most certainly had come to know the love, power and truth with which Jesus taught, and saw the evidence of the authority with which Jesus performed wonderful miracles. Most scholars believe this centurion eventually become a follower of Jesus, maybe clandestinely. Nevertheless, it took courage to openly approach the Master and even a lot of guts to ask Him for a favor.

The centurion got to the heart of the matter when he declared, *"You only have to speak the words that will heal my servant, and what You say will be performed in my servant's body. You don't even have to go to my house to do it which would be in violation of Jewish customs – because You have great authority in You, and Your word is enough."* His simple explanation of how authority works spoke volumes of this man's heart and understanding, and are as relevant today as they were in the first century.

Jesus was very pleased with the centurion's request presented with such faith, and He turned to the disciples to express this. He explained, *"Some people will get this, others – including many of My own – will not."* This is still true today. Many will dismiss the principle of connecting our lives with the promises of God's Word, saying it is just *"name-it-and-claim-it."* That is not what God taught me in 1961, and it is not what I believe today. That is not what I experienced in 1961, and it not what I have experienced countless times over these decades. What I know is that God took a young man who had lots of doubts, was drowning in personal poverty, with sparse results in ministry, and whose heart was timid and lacking faith ... and transformed him into a righteous lion-hearted man who has been used to accomplish great things for God's glory!

*The wicked flee when no man pursueth, but the righteous are bold as a lion.*
**Proverbs 28:1**; KJV

### Bringing It Home

Back at that little rented motel, Joyce was struggling to raise our five children, with her husband mostly away traveling and often down to their last penny. The adage, *"It is no sin to be poor but it is mighty inconvenient"* was always hanging over our heads. She was always a strong prayer-warrior who supported my ministry, often encouraging me when there was no evidence of success. But it was difficult for her.

Just prior to God's revelation of *MY NEVER AGAIN LIST,* I remember how we had spent our last night together before I left on this particular ministry trip. We had gone to bed but couldn't sleep, we were so despondent about our embarrassing financial plight. "What are we going to do?" I wondered. "Should I leave the ministry and get a secular job?" We had been so certain that the move to Canada was in the Lord's will.

Joyce and I spent the whole night talking to God face-to-face, pouring out hearts to Him. I had never heard such a frank, open-hearted prayer as my wife prayed that night. She told the Lord how tired she was of being unable to properly clothe our children, how often we had insufficient food. She told Him how willing she was to live out of a suitcase, to sacrifice without a home, but the deprivations for our children was more than she could bear.

Finally, she prayed, *"Dear God, Supplier of all our needs, You know we have a big problem here. We have very little money. In fact, I don't see how we'll manage this week. Perhaps You no longer want*

*Don to continue in these crusades. If You don't, we'll understand. We are sure that whatever Your reason would be, it would be a good one. Now if You do not meet our financial needs, we will give up this ministry to somebody else. We want whatever You want."*

Like Moses of old, Joyce talked right out of her heart to the Lord. I was totally convinced as was confirmed very shortly that the Heavenly Father was well-pleased with His daughter for talking to Him to freely and unashamedly. Her words and God's promise made the difference. That prayer prepared the way for the tide to turn for us spiritually and financially.

When I returned to Victoria after receiving the life-changing *MY NEVER AGAIN LIST,* I shared this newly-penned testimony with Joyce. She received it gladly. She could already witness that my life had been dramatically changed by these truths, and she was more than willing to be a partaker in what the Lord had done. Joyce caught the contagious spirit of my new faith, and agreed with me that everything would be different now.

It was. Never again were we so poverty-stricken, either in faith or in finances.

*He sent His word and healed them; He rescued them from the grave.*

**Psalm 107:20**; KJV

**Part Two:
HOW IT HAPPENED**
By **Jeanne Gossett Halsey**

## Chapter One: Agreeing With the Word

*"I have told you all this so that you may have peace in Me. Here on Earth you will have many trials and sorrows; but take heart, because I have overcome the world!"*
**John 16:33**; NLT

The key to realizing that God actually has a plan for us and cares intimately about the details of our lives starts by understanding and accepting that His plan has *already* been clearly written out in His Book. Learning to align our lives with His Guide-Book shouldn't be that difficult, but we often trip over ourselves trying to solve our own problems rather than going to the Source of our lives to see what provisions He has *already* made for us.

*"What do you mean? How can the God of the entire Universe care about an individual person?"* That's a common rebuttal but wholly mistaken; Jesus Himself refuted it:

*"What is the price of two sparrows – one copper coin? But not a single sparrow can fall to the ground without your Father knowing it. And the very hairs on your head are all numbered. So don't be afraid;*

*you are more valuable to God than a whole flock of sparrows."*
**Matthew 10:29-31**; NLT

For new believers (and many old tired-out believers) to *learn their rights in Christ* is an important element to becoming vibrant Christians! There is far more to learn and employ as a believer than simply accepting the gift of salvation – *how* we live victoriously through Christ in a world filled with sin and trouble is essential to not just surviving but actually thriving. It is the difference between not only accepting "Jesus as Savior" but accepting "Jesus as Lord" too.

## A Troubled Upbringing

Born in Anadarko, Oklahoma, on July 20, 1929, Donald Edward Gossett came from a non-Christian family. Yes, there were many Christians in his extended family and they prayed for him continually – but his own father, Bob Gossett, was a rough-and-tumble alcoholic who was often abusive to his wife and children. His mother, Jane Gossett, was a

Donald Edward Gossett, around age 18. (1947)

sweet woman who tried to survive her husband's bullying and to protect her children, but she had not yet learned that she had a Savior waiting to enter her life.

Don was born at the beginning of the Great Depression, in one of the economically hardest-hit places in the whole United States; he grew up in poverty.  Bob Gossett was trained as an electrician, and he traveled throughout the southwestern states working with the telephone company, climbing high up the newly-installed network of telephone poles and attaching the spreading electrical wiring.  One day Bob was accidentally handed a "live" wire ... and immediately his whole body was engulfed in high voltage electricity.  He passed out, and fell many feet to rocks on the the ground.  Burned over the majority of his body, his right hand and arm fell away in cinders.  His co-workers and the hastily-called paramedics (such as they had back in the 1930s), who immediately feared for his life.  Through the grace of God, many months later he recovered from the accident, but now his livelihood was taken away.

Life was difficult in the 1930s, and Bob Gossett turned to a variety of types of employment to provide for his wife and three children.  He traveled with a rough sort of friends, some who were involved in illegal activities.  The family lived in 36 different homes during Don's first 18 years of life, and he attended dozens of schools.

Don recalled how they suffered in those years of extreme poverty; how his sister, his brother and himself would eat two bowls of cereal every morning for breakfast but they had to keep the milk from the first bowl to use in the second.  He was a poor boy in a poor family ... and his father's reputation as a gambler, hard drinker (these were the years of Prohibition), womanizing, foul-mouthed, bad-tempered character could not promise a golden future for his family.  (A distant cousin was notorious bank-robber Bonnie Parker, the female half of the murderous team of "Bonnie and Clyde.")

As for his father's character, Don remembered when his parents would argue loudly and physically and often.  Once he had to wrestle his father to the ground to take away the rifle his Dad was pointing at his mother threateningly.  Violence and uncertainty dogged Don's young life; another time, a so-called family friend actually abducted the child Don and held him for ransom.

Don often felt outcast by the townspeople, who disdained Bob Gossett's unsavory lifestyle.  Hungry for a pure life, at the age of 12 Don attended a local camp-meeting, where he responded to Christ's invitation to accept salvation. This did little to change Don's outward life – he still was shunned by local churches because of his father's reputation – but it began a new inner Godly work that would bear much fruit later. Don was joined in his newfound faith by his older sister Donnis; the two siblings often walked long miles to attend a Nazarene church far from their home town.

### **Self-Motivated**

When Don became a Christian, he received very little Bible training; he briefly attended Bible School in San Francisco, but doesn't credit his teachers with greatly impacting his beliefs. He decided to dig into the Word for himself; memorizing long passages in the Bible became one of his personal goals. He was not exposed to much doctrine other than a low-key, passive form of Christianity, but he persevered to live a clean life far removed from the violence and disgrace of his father's example.

Hold that image of the young Don Gossett growing up in the 1930's and 40's ... and move forward to 1961, where he has become an itinerant traveling evangelist, with a loving wife and five small children. He is six-feet tall, he has dark, curly hair, and smiling brown eyes. He is healthy and not afraid to work. But he also is very poor, he is struggling, he has a heart to spread the Gospel ... but his brave preaching doesn't balance with his personal troubles. In his life he has seen God move mightily through evangelists like William W. Freeman and T.L. Osborn (he worked closely with both men), but now he is out on his own ... and seemingly failing:

*"One day, after being away from my family for several days, I was driving back to them ... and I was wallowing in negative, morbid thoughts. I was dejected, disappointed and frustrated over the constant failures and losses in my life and ministry. My personal and family needs were staggering."*

In your mind's eye, see 32-year-old Don away from his family, holding a revival meeting at a small church in Longview, Washington. He is staying at the home of the local pastor. Alone in the guest room, Don takes out his Bible, and reads – as if for the first time! – the fourth chapter of Philippians ... and lands on the thirteenth verse:

*I can do all things through Christ Who strengthens me!*

He reads it out loud once. He reads it out loud twice. He flips to the flyleaf of his Bible and writes the verse there.

This is not the first time God has electrified a single verse from His Word and changed Don's life. In April 1954, when his wife Joyce had suffered for long months with painful Rheumatic Fever, Psalm 27:1 has become a catalyst to her complete healing:

Newlyweds Don and Joyce Gossett. (1950)

*The LORD is my light and my salvation; whom shall I fear? The LORD is the strength of my life; of whom shall I be afraid?*

"*The LORD is the strength of my life*" was an essential promise Don and Joyce relied on for the health and welfare of their family. Don *knew* this was true, but he was still learning how to grasp and apply *all* the promises in God's Word into his life and ministry.

In this supernatural moment of God intensely speaking to him, he presses on. He flips to the book of Matthew, chapter eight. There are two main protagonists in this Bible story: Jesus Christ, and the Roman centurion. Don begins to relate to the plight of the centurion: a man who had a serious, life-threatening need in his family. Don begins to understand that God's authority in his own life needs to be activated by learning to cling to the promises clearly written in the Bible. He needs to speak it out loud so that his heart and mind can hear and apply that sparkling word of truth ... and so that the wicked enemy (see 1 Peter 5:8-9) – who is intent on our destruction – can hear God's Word pouring out of God's servant's mouth.

> *But the officer said, "Lord, I am not worthy to have You come into my home.* ***Just say the word*** *from where You are, and my servant will be healed.*
> **Matthew 8:8**; NLT; emphasis added

Don writes on the flyleaf of his Bible:

#1 - NEVER AGAIN will I confess "I can't," for "I can do all things through Christ which strengtheneth me" (Philippians 4:13). The only thing I cannot do is what I say I cannot do. I can do what God says I can do: "All things through Christ!"

A lightness of heart like he has never known before begins to stir inside Don. He is looking at himself, a man who struggles with self-confidence

... and decides he would rather see himself the way his Heavenly Father sees him through the lens of His own Son: *as a man who can!*

## Cause and Effect

Don surveys his life again and sees the reality of the struggle to provide for his family, the grip of poverty that had plagued his own childhood and still threatens to overwhelm him. A holy rage begins to boil inside him as he visualizes the faces of little Michael (age 10), Judy (9), Jeanne (8), Donnie (6), and Marisa (4), whom he loves so dearly, and for whom he so desperately wants to provide for their well-being. His Heavenly Father, Who knows majestically how to provide for His children, draws Don's attention farther along Philippians 4:

> *And this same God Who takes care of me will supply all your needs from His glorious riches, which have been given to us in Christ Jesus.*
> **Philippians 4:19**; NLT

A flood of Bible verses which he has memorized begins pouring through his heart; one-by-one, they nourish his aching soul:

*The LORD is my Shepherd, I have all that I need.*

**Psalm 23:1**; NLT

*Keep on asking, and you will receive what you ask for. Keep on seeking, and you will find. Keep on knocking, and the door will be opened to you. For everyone who asks, receives. Everyone who seeks, finds. And to everyone who knocks, the door will be opened.*

*You parents if your children ask for a loaf of bread, do you give them a stone instead? Or if they ask for a fish, do you give them a snake? Of course not! So if you sinful people know how to give good gifts to your children, how much more will your Heavenly Father give good gifts to those who ask Him.*

**Matthew 7:7-11**; NLT

*For all the animals of the forest are Mine, and I own the cattle on a thousand hills. I know every bird on the mountains, and all the animals of the field are Mine. If I were hungry, I would not tell you, for all the world is Mine and everything in it.*

*Make thankfulness your sacrifice to God, and keep the vows you made to the Most High. Then call on Me when you are in trouble, and I will rescue you, and you will give Me glory.*
**Psalm 50:10-12, 14-15**; NLT

Don exclaims, *"My Father knows how to give good gifts to me, and He does! I can be the need-fulfilling father that my children need me to be! My Father is unlimited!"* Don writes in his Bible:

**#2 - NEVER AGAIN will I confess lack, for "My God shall supply all my need according to His riches in glory by Christ Jesus" (Philippians 4:19). My supply comes from God, and He never runs out!**

Like the old hymn, *"Joy unspeakable and full of glory"* begins to flow through Don's heart, and he lifts up his voice to sing. This supernatural transformation is changing him from the inside out.

## Chapter Two: Learning Boldness

Often when we read and learn God's Word, a verse or an idea will enter like a seed into our minds but not initially make it all the way to our hearts. There's nothing wrong with that as long as we don't let that seed go completely dormant. In His own timing – and often when we least expect it – God will take a verse previously planted in our hearts and explode it into life!

*Fearing people is a dangerous trap,* but *trusting the LORD means safety.*
**Proverbs 29:25**; NLT

As a child, Don had battled the spirit of fear in many different forms. In childhood, he had an inexplicable fear of people's faces. Whenever visitors came to his home, he would hide away in closets or under a bed. His parents were aware of this childish fear and just tolerated it; as Don grew older, that fear began to

The only time Don Gossett was ever camera-shy. His father Bob Gossett is in the background on the right; his mother Jane Gossett and his sister Donnis Gossett are in the foreground; Don is on the left. (1935)

vanish.

In his teen years, however, fear paralyzed him in a different way. Don was a popular student primarily because of his athletic prowess; in his final year of high school, he was elected to be president of the Student Body. This required him to lead a weekly assembly at the school, with all the teachers and students present. Don lived in absolute dread of that one-hour Student Body assembly.

One of his teachers, Mr. Richardson, called Don aside, "You are a good boy; all the teachers like you, it's obvious the students like you because they elected you overwhelmingly as their Student Body president. But Don, you must overcome this fear of public speaking! You will never go far in life unless you overcome this fear." Don walked away from that meeting with Mr. Richardson wondering if ever in his life he would be able to conquer the fear of public speaking.

After graduation, the Lord brought Don through a tremendous spiritual experience when He laid His hand on Don's life and called him into full-time ministry. It was several more years, however, before Don truly understood where his fears came from and how to overcome them.

It was his wife Joyce who pinpointed Proverbs 29:25 – the verse about *"the fear of man"* – bringing it to Don's attention. Joyce had been raised in the home of a fiery Pentecostal pastor, and she was known for having a fiery Cherokee temper. (Most of the Cherokee tribe had been re-settled in Oklahoma, and both Don and Joyce had Cherokee blood in their heritage.) Don had been raised as a peace-maker in a volatile home, and he saw that similar fiery Cherokee temperament displayed in both his parents; but his earliest training in Christianity was from a mild Baptist perspective. He used to joke: *"The Baptists are known for baptism by water, the Pentecostals are known for baptism by fire. When you put fire and water together, you get steam – and we've been steaming along together all these years."*

*"The LORD is the strength of my life!"* Don and Joyce Gossett, with daughter Jeanne, revisiting the house in Oklahoma where Joyce was healed of Rheumatic Fever. (1963)

Joyce had experienced her own battle with fear. When she was 18, she thought she heard God's voice say, *"Joyce, you will not live to be 21."* For the next eleven months, she endured a daily battle with the fear of death, and only by a tremendous spiritual struggle did she overcome that fear. Years later, because she felt a calling to minister to people suffering with fear, she wrote a book, *"Eleven Lonely Months,"* about her struggle and deliverance. Having been a fear-sufferer herself, Joyce could recognize fear in Don as well, and she was able to minister to him.

There comes a time when being a "man-pleaser" more than a "God-pleaser" creates an overall attitude of timidity and fear. Don had tried to appease men of many denominations and attitudes. For instance, when he had worked as the Editor of a big-time ministry's monthly magazine, he often turned in the last-draft of the publication for his employer's final approval, only to have everything arbitrarily rejected. This led to strenuous all-nighters of re-writing and re-typesetting in order to make the printer's deadline ... all because a temperamental man who made a whimsical (possibly ego-driven, and often inaccurate) decisions. Don wanted to bring his best attitude of working for his employer as if working for Christ (see Colossians 3:22-25), but it also engendered an uncertainty in his own talents and abilities, which led to a thinly-veiled "fear of man."

When Don embarked into his own ministry, a nagging fear followed him: *"Would he ever be 'good enough' to minister with confidence to people, to earn sufficient finances to support his family, to sustain an independent ministry?"* He wrote:

*"I was continually defeated, trounced and routed. I was snared in the trap of my own negative words. I was constantly talking about my defeats and failures ... and I got exactly what I said: more defeats, more failures, more loss of self-esteem."*

In 1961, during this day-long "moment of truth" with God, another verse jumps out at Don with bull's-eye clarity:

*For God has not given us a spirit of fear and timidity, but of power, love and self-discipline.*
**2 Timothy 1:7**; NLV

*"Fear of man?"* Yes, blended with a tumultuous childhood, a series of jobs working with unpredictable employers (who also happened to be effective evangelists), and now evidently failing as an itinerant evangelist, it is no wonder young Don Gossett felt *"snared by fear."* How to overcome fear? Speak God's Word that specifically addresses it! Don writes in his Bible:

## #3 - NEVER AGAIN will I confess fear for "God hath not given me the spirit of fear, but of power, and of love, and of a sound mind" (II Timothy 1:7).

The valuable teaching Don began to receive that day later eventually translated itself into multiple books: *"Fear Power"* ... *"How to Overcome Fear and Live In Victory"* ... and many other titles. Learning to please God rather than man creates a courage, a boldness that worked into his ministry, especially when he began to use the *"gift of healing"* (see 1 Corinthians 12:9-10) in public, and in later years when he risked himself to travel to many foreign nations in ministry. (In 2003, he was officially "blacklisted" from further ministry in India because he was "caught" in public leading thousands of people in the Sinner's Prayer – at least he was actually guilty of being a soul-winner!)

### Boldness Versus Doubt

A favorite Bible passage for Don to minister was from Acts 3 and 4; I think he could visualize himself speaking with boldness just like Peter:

*Peter and John went to the Temple one afternoon to take part in the three o'clock prayer service. As they approached the*

*Temple, a man lame from birth was being carried in. Each day he was put beside the Temple gate, the one called the Beautiful Gate, so he could beg from the people going into the Temple. When he saw Peter and John about to enter, he asked them for some money.*

*Peter and John looked at him intently, and Peter said, "Look at us!" The lame man looked at them eagerly, expecting some money. But Peter said, "I don't have any silver or gold for you. But I'll give you what I have. In the Name of Jesus Christ the Nazarene, get up and walk!" Then Peter took the lame man by the right hand and helped him up. And as he did, the man's feet and ankles were instantly healed and strengthened. He jumped up, stood on his feet, and began to walk! Then, walking, leaping, and praising God, he went into the Temple with them.*

*All the people saw him walking and heard him praising God. When they realized he was the lame beggar they had seen so often at the Beautiful Gate, they were absolutely astounded! They all rushed out in amazement to Solomon's Colonnade, where the man was holding tightly to Peter and John. Peter saw his opportunity and addressed the crowd. "People of Israel," he said, "what is so surprising about this? And why stare at us as though we had made this man walk by our own power or godliness? For it is the God of Abraham, Isaac, and Jacob – the God of all our ancestors – Who has brought glory to His servant Jesus by doing this. This is the same Jesus Whom you handed over and rejected before Pilate, despite Pilate's decision to release Him." ...*

*The members of the Council were amazed* **when they saw the boldness of Peter and John,** *for they could see that they were ordinary men with no special training in the Scriptures. They also recognized them as men who had been with Jesus.*
    **Acts 3:1-13, 4:13**; NLT; emphasis added

If Don was inspired by the personalities, actions and reports of Bible heroes, most likely he admired the Apostle Peter: who was bold, simple (not mendacious), deeply devoted to Jesus Christ, and effective as he shared the Gospel in that first century.

## Dangers of Apathy

Apathy and laziness are dangerous illnesses spreading through the Christian Church. "Passing the buck" (letting someone else do the work, meet the need, take the stand) is a common ailment of modern Western society where self-centeredness is rampant and pervasive, while *"Love your neighbor"* (see Matthew 29:31, also Mark 12:31) fades in importance. This is fundamentally wrong, and it's fair to state that God will judge His people for failing to meet His standard. In Christian circles, this often translates as mediocre faith, a blasé attitude about responsibility to fulfill God's requirements; and it is easy to disguise apathy as "lack of faith" or even outright doubt.

Don's essential personality was influenced by his mother's sweetness and kindness; it is probable he actively refused to be volatile like his father. Being a peace-maker between his parents during their arguments and fights was Don's choice – after all, *"Blessed are the peace makers for theirs is the Kingdom of God"* (Matthew 5:9) – but Don needed boldness as an antidote to doubt, and unfettered faith as an antidote to failure if he was going to be effective as a Christian minister, if he was going to excel in providing for his family.

This principle of overcoming doubt and increasing faith must be applied to lives of all Christians, not just to Don's own need. It *was* his need – it was also the need of those to whom he ministered. On that cross-roads day in 1961, Don writes this in his Bible:

**#4 - NEVER AGAIN will I confess doubt and lack of faith, for "God hath given to every man the measure of faith" (Romans 12:3).**

There was a shift taking place within Don's heart, not just a resolve to become more bold, but an attitude of possibility! God's Word was etched on his heart, enabled through his mind and exhibited in his behavior:

> *Jesus looked at them intently and said, "Humanly speaking, it is impossible. But with God, everything is possible!"*
> **Matthew 19:26**; NLT

In 1967, Rev. Robert H. Schuller (who later became a personal friend of Don's) wrote and published a best-seller, *"Move Ahead With Possibility Thinking."* In 1961, Don Gossett was learning this vital truth – *not* based on a man's own efforts but wholly based on relying on God's ability – through the personal tutelage of the Holy Spirit.

## Chapter Three: Holy Heartburn

The ideal of most people is a strong, successful person, a super-man, an all-wise and infallible person who accomplishes great things for himself (or herself) and for humanity. The antithesis of this is a wimp, a useless, ineffective, constantly-failing, fumbling fool. Western Literature is filled with stories, factual and fictional, of those who have been strong and successful, equally bracketed (often humorously) by those who have been weak and powerless.

Don grew up with many types of people: those who bullied their way to ascendancy ... those who wavered and held back ... those who inspired and encouraged ... those who ridiculed and disdained. When a teenaged Don had tenuously announced to his father that he felt led to become a preacher, his father laughed out loud and derided, "Don, you can't put a sentence together without stuttering. How do you ever expect to get up in front of people and preach?" There it was: that fear of man.

It was true Don Gossett stammered badly, especially when speaking to a group of people. It wasn't that his mind was unable to organize his thoughts but the transition from his mind to his mouth was filled with obstacles caused by nervousness. He excelled as a writer – but as a speaker, he was timid and difficult to understand. He was outgoing and trustworthy, popular among his school friends; but this was more because of his sports-prowess than his public speaking ability. Nevertheless, something was burning inside his heart: a desire to be effective as a witness for Christ Jesus. In later years, he described this as "holy heartburn," based on **Jeremiah 20:9**:

> *But if I say I'll never mention the LORD or speak in His Name,* **His Word burns in my heart like a fire.** *It's like a fire in my bones! I am worn out with trying to hold it in! I can't do it!* (emphasis added)

In 1947, 18-year-old Don had taken an enormous step of faith to withstand the derision of his own father, and to endure the ridicule of people and still choose to stand up in public to speak about the Gospel of Jesus Christ. He began with one-on-one conversations with his school friends; in Bible School, he pushed himself to stand on street corners and declare the Word of God to total strangers. As he stubbornly held to the calling he knew God has written in his heart, an amazing transformation took place: Don's stuttering diminished and then completely vanished. He spoke with clarity and vigor, declaring the Word of the Lord with conviction and persuasion. He began to lead people to Christ, and the more he spoke, the stronger his speech grew.

Why? Because Don had discovered a Bible verse that inspired him:

*But the people who know their God will be strong and will resist [the enemy].*
**Daniel 11:32b**; NLT

It was God's Word of encouragement that enabled Don to speak and teach the Gospel without speech impediment. The inherent weakness of a human being struggling with a speech impediment was overturned by the undying truth of the Bible ... and young Don Gossett began to be a powerful soul-winner!

As he sits in that Longview pastor's home in 1961, these memories of successfully overcoming adversity fill his heart with courage. It is important for all believers to regularly renew their minds with thoughts of what God has already done in their lives; we call it "counting your blessings." God had instructed His people the Israelites to regularly recall His great deeds among them:

*In that wonderful day you will sing: "Thank the LORD! Praise His Name! Tell the nations what He has done. Let them know how mighty He is!"*

**Isaiah 12:4**; NLT

This memory of God's strength over his own weakness prompts Don to write in his Bible:

**#5 - NEVER AGAIN will I confess weakness, for "The LORD is the strength of my life" (Psalm 7:1; KJV) and "The people that know their God shall be strong and do exploits" (Daniel 11:32).**

Many years later, Don Gossett's firstborn grandson Alexander Halsey (son of his daughter Jeanne) committed his life to full-time ministry of the Gospel of Jesus Christ, just like his grandfather. However, Alex also suffered with a difficult speech impediment from childhood, and his prospects to become an effective minister of the Gospel were murky. Don prayed for his grandson to be

Don Gossett introducing his grandson Alexander Halsey, at a Partner Meeting. (2007)

delivered from stuttering; those prayers were underscored by family and friends.

In 2005, Jeanne Halsey visited Alex at the *Youth With A Mission* Base in Lonavala, Maharashtra, India, where Alex was teaching the *School of Biblical Studies* (a 9-month thorough inductive study of the Bible). Sitting as a guest at the back of the classroom, she marveled to hear her 24-year-old son expounding on the intricacies of the Bible without a stammer or a hitch, speaking with authority and conviction, teaching these eager students to understand and absorb God's Holy Word. That miraculous healing God had done for her father all those years ago was duplicated here for her son these many years later! It is God's gift to His anointed ones.

## Militant Christianity

In the life of every Christian there are two internal influences: the voice of God our Father, and the voice of Satan our enemy. Learning to distinguish these voices can be a lifelong lesson, especially because Satan tries very hard to disguise himself. God loves us and protects us eternally, but Satan is fighting against us through all the days of our lives. When a naïve believer becomes complacent and erroneously believes they are exempt from Satanic attack, trouble upon trouble will mount in their lives.

How that misguided perception can even develop is a mystery! It is a delusion that Satan has mounted against God's people for generations, with varying success. He has warped our understanding of God's Word, throwing blindness into our minds so that we do not need to stay sharp and prepared for the attacks of our enemy. In this clearly defined passage, notice the original verbs are all in the "present and future tenses":

> *A final word:* Be *strong in the Lord and in His mighty power.* Put on *all of God's armor so that you* will *be able to stand firm against all strategies of the devil.* For we are *not fighting against flesh-and-blood enemies, but against evil rulers and authorities of the unseen world, against mighty powers in this dark world, and against evil spirits in the heavenly places.*
>
> *Therefore,* put on *every piece of God's armor so you* will *be able to resist* the *enemy in the time of evil.* Then after the *battle you* will still be standing *firm.* Stand *your ground,* putting on *the belt of truth and the body armor of God's*

*righteousness. For shoes,* put on *the peace that comes from the Good News so that you* will be fully prepared. *In addition to all of these,* hold up *the shield of faith to stop the fiery arrows of the devil.* Put on *salvation as your helmet, and* take *the sword of the Spirit, which is the Word of God.*

Pray *in the Spirit at all times and on every occasion.* Stay alert *and* be persistent *in your prayers for all believers everywhere. And* pray *for me too.* Ask *God to* give *me the right words so I can boldly explain God's mysterious plan that the Good News is for Jews and Gentiles alike. I am in chains now, still preaching this message as God's ambassador. So* pray *that I will keep on speaking boldly for Him, as I should.*

**Ephesians 6:10-20**; NLT; emphasis added

How can we mistake that "call to arms" to enter the *active* battlefield?  God has already equipped us with strong weapons – He never once tells us to sit down in comfort and let the world go to Hell without us because He will hold us safely away from all harm and danger!  He has promised to comfort us in our difficulty (see Psalm 46:1) ... to walk with us through death and loss (see Psalm 23:4) ... to renew our strength when we are depleted (see Isaiah 40:31) ... to always be with us (see Deuteronomy 31:16) ... *and* He has promised to give us the strategies to overcome our enemy (see Psalm 144:1) ... to fully and properly equip us with armor and weapons (see Ephesians 6:10-20) ... and to lead us in the victory parade (see 2 Corinthians 2:14). We are not called to "passive Christianity" – we are enlisted in the active, militant Army of God!

We know a lot about our enemy. We know where he originated (see Ezekiel 28:12-19) ... what caused his fall (Isaiah 14:12-15) ... where he is now (see 2 Corinthians 11:14-15) ... that we are to actively oppose him (see 1 Peter 5:8-10) ... what his history has been (Colossians 2:15) ... and that his final fate is already determined (see Revelation 20:10). We know he hates us and will do anything and everything he can to destroy us. None of his attacks against us should be feared because **we are already equipped to defeat him:**

> *Then there was war in Heaven. Michael and his angels fought against the dragon and his angels. And the dragon lost the battle, and he and his angels were forced out of Heaven. This great dragon – the ancient serpent called the devil or Satan, the one deceiving the whole world – was*

*thrown down to the earth with all his angels.*

*Then I heard a loud voice shouting across the heavens: "It has come at last – salvation and power, and the Kingdom of our God, and the authority of His Christ. For the accuser of our brothers and sisters has been thrown down to Earth – the one who accuses them before our God day and night. And they have defeated him by the blood of the Lamb and by their testimony; and they did not love their lives so much that they were afraid to die.*

*"Therefore, rejoice, O heavens! And you who live in the heavens, rejoice! But terror will come on the earth and the sea, for the devil has come down to you in great anger, knowing that he has little time."*
        **Revelation 12:7-12**; NLT; emphasis added

Don is familiar with the taunting threats and destructive nature of our great enemy, and he is becoming more intentional and courageous about standing firmly on God's Word against Satanic onslaught. In later years, he will stand before thousands in India, watching demon-possessed people writhing in torment ... then with supernatural boldness, speak firmly against those

Don Gossett praying for the sick, in India. (2000)

tormentors and, with the authority of the Name of Jesus, cast them out! What he was learning with intensity in 1961 would remain with him for the remainder of his life and ministry. He writes in his Bible:

**#6 - NEVER AGAIN will I confess supremacy of Satan over my life, for "Greater is He that is within me than he that is in the world" (I John 4:4).**

That day, Don's total character and personality are being transformed by the Word of God!

## Chapter Four: Born to Conquer

God did not create competition. Competition comes from one person thinking he is better than another person, and so he sets out to prove it. Or perhaps he thinks he is not as good as the other person, so he sets out to destroy the other person in an effort to make himself somehow better. Only when "healthy competition" causes both persons to be improved and brought to a mutually better situation could competition be spun around to be a "good thing."

### Know Your Enemy

The very nature of competition demands a winner and a loser. One who is above and one who is below. For many people, life seems to be one defeat after another. This skewed perspective is one of Satan's favorites to use, especially against those who believe in Jesus Christ. It is the same he tried to use against Jesus Christ Himself during those forty days in the wilderness:

> *Then Jesus was led by the Spirit into the wilderness to be tempted there by the devil. For forty days and forty nights, He fasted and became very hungry. During that time, the devil came and said to Him,*

*"If You are the Son of God, tell these stones to become loaves of bread."*

*But Jesus told him, "No! The Scriptures say, 'People do not live by bread alone, but by every word that comes from the mouth of God.'"*

*Then the devil took Him to the Holy City, Jerusalem, to the highest point of the Temple, and said, "If You are the Son of God, jump off! For the Scriptures say: 'He will order His angels to protect You. And they will hold You up with their hands so You won't even hurt Your foot on a stone.'"*

*Jesus responded, "The Scriptures also say, 'You must not test the Lord your God.'"*

*Next the devil took Him to the peak of a very high mountain and showed Him all the kingdoms of the world and their glory. "I will give it all to You," he said, "if You will kneel down and worship me."*

*"Get out of here, Satan," Jesus told him. "For the Scriptures say: 'You must worship the Lord your God and serve only Him.'" Then the devil went away, and angels came*

*and took care of Jesus.*
**Matthew 4:1-11; NLT**

The self-generated sin of pride led to a contest, a competition, between the Son of God and the one who previously was His best friend in Heaven: Lucifer, now known as Satan.

*How are you fallen from Heaven, O shining star, son of the morning! You have been thrown down to the Earth, you who destroyed the nations of the world. For you said to yourself, "I will ascend to Heaven and set my throne above God's stars. I will preside on the mountain of the gods far away in the north. I will climb to the highest heavens and be like the Most High." Instead, you will be brought down to the place of the dead, down to its lowest depths.*
**Isaiah 14:12-15; NLT**

*You were the model of perfection, full of wisdom and exquisite in beauty. You were in Eden, the Garden of God. ... I ordained and anointed you as the mighty angelic guardian. You had access to the holy Mountain of God and walked among the stones of fire. You were blameless in all you did from the day you were created, until the day evil was found in you. Your rich commerce led you to violence, and you sinned. So I banished you in disgrace from the Mountain of God. I expelled you, O mighty guardian, from your place among the stones of fire. Your heart was filled with pride because of all your beauty. Your wisdom was corrupted by your love of splendor. So I threw you to the ground and exposed you ... So I brought fire out from within you, and it consumed you. I reduced you to ashes on the ground in the sight of all who were watching. All who knew you are appalled at your fate. You have come to a terrible end, and you will exist no more.*

**Ezekiel 24:12-13, 14-9**

Satan decided to compete against God for the Throne of Heaven, which led to a fierce battle that resulted in one-third of all the angels being defeated and cast out of Heaven (see Revelations 12:4). Pride that leads to competition is not God's plan for His people. However, because Satan continues to roam over the Earth, spreading his wickedness and sin, God sent His own Son to be our Defender! Like the shepherd-boy David coming against the giant Goliath (see 1 Samuel 17), Jesus the Good Shepherd chose to enter the fight as our Defender against Satan the Deceiver

... and He wins!

How Satan works against God's people is the classic struggle we all endure. We can be defeated by the devil, or we can overcome him – but we cannot overcome him in our own strength! When we align ourselves with God's chosen Defender (Jesus Christ), when we live by the wisdom of God's Battle Strategy (the Word of God), when we proclaim that Jesus Christ is Lord over every circumstance of our lives, then the enemy is defeated and his stranglehold is broken. Or as the saying goes, *"We live to fight another day."* **Knowing our rights in Christ is critically important to becoming a successful Christian.**

These timeless truths were facing 31-year-old Don Gossett that day in Longview. He felt a compulsion to learn Christ-like boldness when encountering the works of Satan, and he desired to be a Christ-like winner of the contests between our enemy and ourselves. Too often had he felt defeated or undermined by the enemy's schemes, but the gift of faith within him began to rise like yeast in dough instead of deflating in defeat. He researched the Scriptures that emphasized how often God brought His people out of difficult circumstances through His mighty power, and the "attitude of gratitude" was growing within him.

## Not Born to be Defeated

Don knows that, like it or not, life is a struggle, a competition against difficult odds, and it was his desire to be the winner of the fight! During his school years, Don was always active in sports: baseball, basketball, football, track and field. He knew the value of being a team-player, of following the instructions of his coaches, and of knowing the strengths and weaknesses of his opponents. There was a Bible verse that kept coming to him which had overtones of his experiences in sports, like the parade of athletes who march as a team in the international Olympic Games; years later, gifted writer Eugene Peterson wrote it this way in his Bible translation *The Message:*

Don loved this photo of himself emerging from the Empty Tomb in Jerusalem. (1975)

*In the Messiah, in Christ, God leads us from place to place in one perpetual victory parade.*
**2 Corinthians 2:14**; MSG

Don could see God as his Coach, with Jesus Christ the Star Athlete, and himself a humble member of God's team.  The endless competitions against Satan and his evil team take many forms:  sickness, lack, worry, fear, insecurity ... and Don faces all these issues in his own life and in his family, and he knows that the people to whom he is ministering are experiencing the same kind of defeats.  He writes in the flyleaf of his Bible:

**#7:  NEVER AGAIN will I confess defeat, for "God always causeth me to triumph in Christ Jesus" (II Corinthians 2:14).**

With a flourish, he is preparing his heart to defeat the enemy!

### Obtaining Wisdom From God

Don knows that more people are plagued by the phrase *"I can't"* than almost any other statement in life.  As he studies God's Word, he finds verse after verse, story after story, that relates how God's servants survive and thrive because of His Holy Spirit within them.  He reads about those who accomplish tremendous victories against insurmountable odds because they choose to believe what God says about them rather than what their circumstances seem to reveal.  Then he looks at his own life – at the mistakes he has made, the failures he has experienced, the hand-to-mouth existence he and his family are seemingly stuck in – and he wants it all to change. So that "secret" ingredient to overcoming failure, to making poor decisions, to barely surviving *has to be* in The Book!

> *For I can do everything through Christ, Who gives me strength.*
> **Philippians 4:13**; NLT

He comes to a series of revelations:

- *"No where in the Bible is the phrase 'I can't.' I must learn to speak God's language, to harmonize with Heaven by affirming God's Word, by agreeing with God by agreeing with His Word!"*

- One of his chief worries has been sickness: *"Boldly I will speak it, I can receive my healing for with His stripes I am healed. I can receive my healing because Jesus said 'they shall lays hands on the sick and they shall recover;' hands have been laid on me, thus I am recovering!"*

- Financial lack is another big problem: *"I will declare that I can pay my bills because 'my God shall supply all my needs according to His riches in glory by Christ Jesus!' I have honored God by paying my tithes and giving offerings in His Name, and He says He will 'open Heaven's windows to pour out overflowing blessings, and He will rebuke the devourer for my sake.' I can pay my bills because my God supplies the money to meet every need of my life!"*

As he finds Scriptural "antidotes" for the "maladies" of his life, Don's whole attitude begins to change. He is leaving the world of a "suffering saint" to become a "powerhouse for God"! His earthly mind-set is changing to embrace Christ-like wisdom for how to live his life by the promises of the Word. Two Bible promises really stand out:

*God has united you with Christ Jesus. For our benefit God made Him to be wisdom itself. Christ made us right with God; He made us pure and holy, and He free us from sin.*
**1 Corinthians 1:30**; NLT

*For who can know the Lord's thoughts? Who knows enough to teach him? But we understand these things, for* **we have the mind of Christ.**
**1 Corinthians 2:16**; NLT; emphasis added

Don writes in his Bible:

**#8: NEVER AGAIN** will I confess lack of wisdom, for "Christ Jesus is made unto me wisdom from God" (I Corinthians 1:30).

The heavily-burdened man who bade farewell to his wife and children goodbye a few short days before is not the same man who is going to return to them in another day or two!

## Chapter Five: **The Biggest Enemy**

In his ministry he had encountered people with a variety of physical illness, and he so wanted to be used by God as an agent to deliver healing. The same compassion which so often came upon Jesus Christ during His years on Earth was like a fire in Don's heart, and it motivated him to reach out to others.

Most of his life, Don had experienced excellent health. But there had been an earlier time when his doctor gave him a negative report: he had a critically enlarged heart that endangered his life. Only through the fearless prayers of family and friends did Don overcome this life-threatening issue, and went on to fulfill his destiny in God.

Health challenges were often the most obvious problems plaguing his family. It was because of his mother's life-threatening illness that a teenaged Don took his unsaved parents to an evangelistic crusade conducted by Rev. W.W. Freeman, in Portland, Oregon. There Rev. Freeman prayed over Jane Gossett, and she was instantly healed; shortly thereafter, his parents each accepted Christ as their personal Savior. When Don first met his future wife, Joyce Shackelford, she had already been through a trying ordeal of battling a nervous disorder; she suffered from the fear of dying, and was miraculously healed through the prayers of her maternal grandmother.

### Healing Is Still For Today

Don knew that the same Heavenly Father of the Bible was still in the business of physically healing people today. He had witnessed amazing miracles of people instantly delivered from obvious diseases – deafness, blindness, malignant growths, lame people walking – and he wanted to improve his "skills" as an anointed minister of the Gospel who practiced the gift of healing:

> *The same Spirit gives great faith to another, and to someone else the Spirit gives* ***the gift of healing.***
> **1 Corinthians 12:9**; NLT; emphasis added

*Are any of you sick? You should call for the elders of the church to come and pray over you, anointing you with oil in the Name of the Lord. Such* ***a***

Don praying for the sick in Martinique, French West Indies. (1970)

*prayer offered in faith will heal the sick, and the Lord will make you well. And if you have committed any sins, you will be forgiven.*
**James 5:14-15**; NLT; emphasis added

Don "proving" a healing miracle in India; his second wife Debbie is on the right.

*A spiritual gift is given to each of us so we can help each other. To one person the Spirit gives the ability to give wise advice; to another the same Spirit gives a message of special knowledge. The same Spirit gives great faith to another, and to someone else the one Spirit gives* **the gift of healing. He gives one person the power to perform miracles,** *and another the ability to prophesy. He gives someone else the ability to discern whether a message is from the Spirit of God or from another spirit. Still another person is given the ability to speak in unknown languages, while another is given the ability to interpret what is being said. It is the one and only Spirit Who distributes all these gifts. He alone decides which gift each person should have.*
**1 Corinthians 12:7-11**; NLT; emphasis added

*All of you together are Christ's Body, and each of you is a part of it. Here are some of the parts God has appointed for the church: first are apostles, second are prophets, third are teachers, then those who do miracles, those who have* **the gift of healing,** *those who can help others, those who have the gift of leadership, those who speak in unknown languages. Are we all apostles? Are we all prophets? Are we all teachers? Do we all have the power to do miracles? Do we all have* **the gift of healing?** *Do we all have the ability to speak in unknown languages? Do we all have the ability to interpret unknown languages? Of course not! So you should earnestly desire the most helpful gifts.*
  **1 Corinthians 12:27-31;** NLT; emphasis added

With such clear teaching on the gift of healing active today, Don purposes in his heart to yield himself to God as a conduit of His divine healing. He writes in his Bible:

9th: NEVER AGAIN will I confess sickness, for "With His stripes, I am healed" (Isaiah 53:5; KJV) and "Jesus Himself took my infirmities and bare my sicknesses" (Matthew 8:17).

## Five Reasons to Worry

Don and Joyce Gossett birthed five children within seven years. If anyone had reason to worry, it had to be because of these five lively responsibilities!

Don Gossett's children (left to right): Jeanne ... Michael ... Donnie ... Judy ... Marisa. (1960)

Parenting seemed to come quite naturally to Don and Joyce because their five little children were able to endure the rigors of the nomadic life of traveling evangelists and still be fairly normal kids. They were well-behaved, fully capable of dealing with public church-life – they were quite popular when they sang Gospel songs in their father's public meetings, and their abilities to quote Bible verses on demand was formidable in ones so young – and they believed in their father's representation of having a "sense of adventure" about their travels. To Michael, Judy, Jeanne, Donnie, and Marisa, it was perfectly normal to physically "reside" in their 1956 *Buick* as they traveled all over the United States and Canada; it was typical for them to weekly meet and interact with strangers with confidence ... and they had absolutely no idea that they were poor!

They were all together as a family, their father was pursuing the work of God's ministry, they witnessed people's lives being changed by their father's preaching and healing ministry, and – by the strength of their parents' faith – they were sheltered and protected from the uncertainties of life.

It must have taken extreme measures for Don and Joyce to be able to represent to their young children that life was good because God was good to them.  As Don said it:

> Back at that little rented motel, Joyce was struggling to raise our five children with her husband mostly away traveling and often down to their last penny.  The adage, *"It is no sin to be poor but it is mighty inconvenient"* was always hanging over our heads.  She was always a strong prayer-warrior who supported my ministry, often encouraging me when there was no evidence of success.  But it was difficult for her.

Don faces an avalanche of worry and frustration!  He knows he can not continue living the way he is living – it is unfair to his wife, unfair to his children – and he is ready to leave the ministry.  But this day in October 1961, God says, *"My son Don, I have **already** promised you rescue from your worries and frustrations.  Go to My Book and read it there.  Know from the bottom of* *your soul that **I CARE FOR YOU!** I care about every hair on your head, I care about every mouthful of food you give your children, I care about the rigors your wife endures, I care about the gasoline for your car so you can travel to minister for Me. I care about it all! TRUST ME, Don, and you will begin to see My abundance!"*

God's promise is clearly written in His Book, and is exactly what Don needs to absorb. He writes in his Bible:

**10th: NEVER AGAIN will I confess worries and frustrations, for I am "Casting all my cares upon Him Who careth for Me" (I Peter 5:7). In Christ, I am "care-free"!**

On the road ahead, Don would again and again come to critical moments when worry and frustration would attempt to overwhelm his life. Again and again, Don would take up his Bible to refresh his soul with God's beautiful promise. *"Casting his care"* upon God soon became second-nature to Don Gossett, and was a quality that infiltrated his entire being and added fuel to his formidable faith.

## Chapter Six: **Unlocking Chains**

When he was a child, Don witnessed many of his father's addictions: gambling, smoking cigarettes, alcohol, infidelity, violently unleashing an angry temperament. As much as he loved his father, he was also ashamed of his reckless, God-less behavior.

When he became a Christian and began to study God's Word, he learned an important truth: his physical body was not his own but was on loan to him for a season (lifetime) by He Who had created that body.

> *Don't you realize that your body is the temple of the Holy Spirit, Who lives in you and was given to you by God?* **You do not belong to yourself,** *for God bought you with a high price. So you must honor God with your body.*
>   **1 Corinthians 6:19-20**; NLT; emphasis added

Don had seen the physical and emotional devastation that addictive behaviors caused in his own family. As a young man, he vowed to remain sexually pure throughout his life, including faithfulness to his wife; to the end of his days, he never strayed from that vow. Yet sexual promiscuity and abnormality have become the norm in our society today: marriages crash on the rocks of divorce ... unwanted pregnancies are legally destroyed ... homosexuality is rampant ... pornography is widespread. Don came to see all these behaviors – and many other forms of addiction, such as narcotics, criminal activities, unstable personalities – as the vile works of Satan. He knew these problems pervaded the lives of Christians too, and he searched for God's way to free His people.

Early in their marriage, Don had learned from Joyce some of the principles of prayer and praise that would transform his life. He learned that prayer and praise are the two wings of spiritual power:

> *Be anxious for nothing, but in everything* **by prayer and supplication, with thanksgiving,** *let your requests be made known to God.*
> **Philippians 4:6**; NKJV; emphasis added

> *Continue earnestly* **in prayer,** *being vigilant in it* **with thanksgiving.**
> **Colossians 4:2**; NKJV; emphasis added

Then came the strongest, clearest revelation:

*But Thou are holy, O Thou Who inhabits the praises of Israel.*
**Psalm 22:3**; NKJV

Don wanted greater understanding, so he read that verse again in the Amplified Bible:

*But You are holy, O You Who dwells in [the holy place where] the praises of Israel [are offered].*

It dawned on him: "God actually lives *in my praises! His House, His residence, His preferred place to be anywhere in the Universe and beyond is in the place where I sing my wholehearted praises!*" In the presence of God, sin cannot stand:

*O LORD my God, my Holy One, You Who are eternal – surely You do not plan to wipe us out? ... You are pure and cannot stand the sight of evil.*
**Habakkuk 1:12-13a**; NLT

*See how very much our Father loves us, for He calls us His children, and that is what we are! But the people who belong to this world don't recognize that we are God's children because they don't know Him. Dear friends, we are already God's children, but He has not yet shown us what we will be like when Christ appears. But we do know that we will be like Him, for we will see Him as He really is. And all who have this eager expectation will keep themselves pure, just as He is pure.*

*Everyone who sins is breaking God's law, for all sin is contrary to the law of God. And you know that Jesus came to take away our sins, and there is no sin in Him. Anyone who continues to live in Him will not sin. But anyone who keeps on sinning does not know Him or understand Who He is.*

*Dear children, don't let anyone deceive you about this: When people do what is right, it shows that they are righteous, even as Christ is righteous. But when people keep on sinning, it shows that they belong to the devil, who has been sinning since the beginning. But the Son of God came to destroy the works of the devil. Those who have been born into God's family do not make a practice of sinning, because God's life is in them. So they can't keep on sinning, because they are children of God. So now we can tell who are children of God and who are children of the devil. Anyone*

*who does not live righteously and does not love other believers does not belong to God.*
**1 John 3:1-10**; NLT

Don became convinced that people who saturate themselves in the presence of God – worshipping Him with whole hearts, following His path, dedicated to His service – would be better able to withstand the trials and temptations of addictive behavior than those who linger on the outer edges of having a healthy relationship with Christ.  Not that Christians never make mistakes or fall down, but they choose to immediately throw themselves on God's mercy and draw on His strength to overcome sin.

A "byproduct" of living in God's presence with hearts filled with gratitude, thanksgiving, praise, and worship is that *sin is unwelcome there*.  In fact, Don came to believe that *Satan is allergic to hearing the sound of believers praising and worshipping God,* and he would not be able to get into "firing range" to inflict them with his evil intentions when their eyes are firmly fixed on their Savior and they invite Him into their lives with songs of pure praise.

In years to come, Don would study the principles of praise even more deeply, and write

Front cover of a book Don would write in later years, *"Praise Walk."*

such classics as *"Praise Power," "The Gift of Praise," "Walking, Leaping and Praising God," "Praise Avenue," "The Praise Walk."*

In his Bible, Don writes:

11th: NEVER AGAIN will I confess bondage, for "Where the Spirit of the Lord is, there is liberty" (II Corinthians 3:17). My body is the temple of the Holy Spirit!

*"Walking with God by agreeing with God, and disagreeing with Satan"* was becoming Don's lifelong choice!

### *"No Condemnation"*

From his own youth, when doubts and fears had overwhelmed him and caused him to stutter, Don knew exactly what it felt like to be rejected and condemned. From his earlier experiences of working with temperamental preachers who often let their egos get in the way of their ministry, Don knew exactly what it felt like to be abused and maligned. It's not that he was a sin-full person who spent a lot of time rehashing his previous sins, but his rise from the "unwelcome son of that gambler Bob Gossett" to the "honored man of God" meant that he knew the pain of condemnation.

Many Christians start out believing that once they commit their lives to Christ, they are forever shielded from Satan's attacks. This is very, very wrong thinking, and nearly guarantees that Satan has established a foothold of wrong thinking in their lives. Jesus Himself told us that our lives are not going to be easy:

*"I have told you all this so that you may have peace in Me. Here on Earth you will have many trials and sorrows. But take heart, because I have overcome the world!"*
**John 16:33**; NLT

Paul the Apostle later wrote about this:

*God blesses those who patiently endure testing and temptation. Afterward they will receive the crown of life that God has promised to those who love Him.*
**James 1:12**; NLT

We don't have to be condemned by past or present sins – we must, however, cling to God's promises to *go with us* through the trials of life:

*Even when I walk through the darkest valley, I will not be afraid for You are close beside me.*
**Psalm 23:4**; NLT

No matter what our past sins have been, once they are washed under the saving blood of Jesus Christ, they are *gone*:

*For His unfailing love toward those who fear Him is as great as the height of the Heavens above the Earth. He has removed our sins as far from us as the East is from the West.*
**Psalm 103:11-12**; NLT

"Condemnation" is a trick of the enemy, but we don't have to buckle under that:

*For God has said, "I will never fail you. I will never abandon you." So we can say with confidence, "The Lord is my Helper, so I will have no fear. What can mere people do to me?"*
**Hebrews 13:5b-6**; NLT

Letting go of the past … refusing to permit Satan any access to our lives in the present … standing firmly on God's promises of His strength and protection – these are the steps that enable us to overcome the weight of condemnation. Don knows this will make a difference in his life, and he knows it will make a difference in the lives of those to whom he ministers, so he writes in his Bible:

12th: NEVER AGAIN will I confess condemnation, for "There is therefore now no condemnation to them which are in Christ Jesus" (Romans 8:1). I am in Christ therefore I am free from condemnation!

In October 1961, the new-and-greatly-improved Don Gossett closes his Bible, lays down his pen, rises to his feet, raises his hands to Heaven, and begins a Praise March around the guest bedroom of that pastor's home in Longview, Washington. He cannot wait to get back to Joyce and share this wonderful new lifestyle with her!

*Bold Bible Living!* Don and Joyce Gossett. (1970)

# Epilogue: *Bold Bible Living*

[AUTHOR'S NOTE: To bring to life the ways MY NEVER AGAIN LIST immediately impacted my parents and our family, permit me to reprise a portion of Chapter 3 from my book, *"Stubborn Faith: Celebrating Joyce Gossett,"* where I recounted the "first fruits" of this radical new teaching which Dad had received from God.]

When once more Don returned to Victoria, what a happy reunion it was with his family. Later that evening, after the children were asleep, he shared his newly-penned MY NEVER AGAIN LIST with his wife. Joyce received it gladly. She could readily see Don's whole life had been dramatically changed by these truths, and she was more than willing to be a partaker in what the Lord had done. Joyce caught the contagious spirit of his new faith, and agreed with him that everything would be different now.

When the opportunity arose in 1961 to air a daily 15-minute program from *Radio KARI*, a Christian radio station based in Birch Bay, Washington (just south of the metropolis of Vancouver, British Columbia), Don and Joyce determined they would have easier access to the radio station if they lived on the Mainland of British Columbia rather than on Vancouver Island.

They packed again and moved to modest, affordable lodgings in Vancouver, at the *Peacock Motor Motel* on Kingsway. The three older children enrolled in *Sir Guy Carleton School*, and Joyce cared for toddler Donnie and baby Marisa at home while Don continued to work as an evangelist.

While they had earlier been traveling in Manitoba, the Gossetts met and ministered with Lester and Thelma Pritchard, who pastored a large church in Winnipeg. Later, Rev. Pritchard was offered the pastorate of the prestigious *Evangelistic Tabernacle* in Vancouver, and he invited Don and Joyce to come for extended crusades there. After several weeks of effective ministry at "the Tab," Pastor Pritchard offered them the pastorate of their satellite church, *Surrey Evangelistic Tabernacle* on Townline Road.

Surrey was a developing suburb of Vancouver, and seemed a good place to put down roots for their family. With $100 in their pockets, Don, Joyce and the children set out to find a house to rent in Surrey. After a few hours of looking, they drove by a lovely empty house with a sign in front: *For Sale or Trade; Any Offer Considered.* They turned the car around, drove back to the house, parked in the driveway, and sat looking at this beautiful home. Then Don walked to the nearest house, made inquiry, and subsequently obtained the house-key from a neighbor lady.

They unlocked the front door and walked inside. After strolling through the spacious two floors, four-bedroom house for a few minutes, Joyce spoke, "Honey, the Lord tells me this is going to be our home!" She had a prophetic vision: she was seeing her family living in this home.

Don challenged this statement, thinking mostly of their limited resources of only $100. "Are you sure it's the Holy Spirit Who told you that, or is that just the desire of your own spirit?"

Joyce was exuberant with assurance as she repeated, "I just know this is going to be our home!" So convinced was Joyce that she had heard from God, she went around the outside and inside of the house laying her hands on the walls, the doors, the windows, and claiming it all in the Name of Jesus.

The next day, they contacted the owners and told them of their interest in the house. They asked if they could lease the house for one year, with an option to purchase. A few days later, the principal owner called back, "Rev. Gossett, my partner and I feel that you and your family are the right ones for that house. It won't be necessary to lease it for one year – we are ready to sell it to you now." He continued, "If you will pay $100 down right now and arrange to pay $900 within 90 days, you can move into that house right away. We will draw up the papers to make that house your home."

How their hearts rejoiced as they took those daring steps of faith. In order to hold their hearts steady, Don and Joyce often affirmed *MY NEVER AGAIN LIST.* Those powerful truths fortified their spirits, whereby they were *"walking on the water"* with Jesus, anticipating His miracles daily. It was almost like a dream when they met with the owners in Vancouver, signed the papers and took legal possession of that home in Surrey. By God's grace and mercy, they were able to purchase this

**The Don Gossett Family** (left to right): Joyce ... Jeanne ... Michael ... Marisa ... Judy ... Donnie ... Don (1962)

home; the entire Gossett family felt like they had moved into a castle! Before 1988, the house was completely paid off – and Don and Joyce Gossett never missed a payment.

[Reprinted from *"Stubborn Faith: Celebrating Joyce Gossett,"* by Jeanne M. Halsey; copyright © 2011; published by *ReJoyce Books*, a division of *Masterpieces In Progress Publishing House*; all rights reserved; used with permission.]

# Part Three:
# TESTIMONIALS and TRIBUTES
## By Various Authors

# TESTIMONIALS and TRIBUTES

[AUTHOR'S NOTE: I asked family and friends to comment on Dad's *MNAL*, how it impacted their lives when they first heard this seminal message, how it has held them through the years as they have practiced *"agreeing with God and disagreeing with the devil."* Most commented directly on the message but many more shared warm thoughts on the character of my father, especially as we memorialized and celebrated his life.]

- Praying for you and the Gossett family. I only got to know your Dad through you and Judy, but I treasure those times. He must have been a wonderful man. What a Godly heritage! ~ **Lola Allen;** Edmond, Oklahoma

- I pray God's comfort on your family. I enjoyed working for him in the office, years ago. Great memories of his positive preaching, especially "the attitude of gratitude." ~ **Kristel Loland Asmus;** Bowling Green, Ohio

- A very special person; just think about the party they are having in Heaven! Lots of love to you all. Grandpa God was a very loving, kind, thoughtful person. He will be missed by so many. God received a wonderful angel today. God bless! ~ **Michelle** (*née* McDonald) **Bakker;** Blaine, Washington

# Life Radically Transformed
By **Rev. John Barker**
Langley, British Columbia

I was raised in a poor family. My mother was a cripple, and our family had little money. I went to school with holes in my pants and shoes, was laughed at by the kids, always picked last for the sports teams. I grew up with low self-esteem.

As the years went by, I married, fathered two boys, and did my best to provide for my family. Then my marriage fell apart, and I found myself alone, living in my small office, because my wife had found someone else to love. I was devastated to lose my wife and our boys; I became focused on the pain and betrayal, and plotted to murder the lover she had found. I kept saying, "I'm a loser, I'm a loser! I've lost my Dad, lost my Mom, lost my wife, lost my kids, and now I'm about to lose my job."

I drank to ease the pain; I couldn't start my day without a stiff drink. For about a year, I lived in my small office, and slowly sank into despair. I knew I was about to sink even lower because I was working on an ignition bomb to kill my ex-wife's lover. I was desperate for help! One night, in a drunken stupor, feeling all alone and not wanting to live, I cried, "God – if there is a God – I need help!" Then I fell into a deep drunken sleep.

God heard my despairing cry for help and began to reveal a turn in my road of life. I just happened to tune into the KARI radio station ... and I heard Don

Gossett for the first time. He was sharing about his new book, *"What You Say Is What You Get."* This caught my attention – a spark of hope in my dark world! Then I heard Don's *"My Never Again List."* This was the catalyst for my turn-around.

I realized I had been quoting words from sad songs like: *"Born to lose / And now I'm losing you,"* which was reinforcing my perspective that I was a loser. But then I read Don's *"My Never Again List"* and began speaking: *"Never again will I confess fear, for God has not given me the spirit of fear, but of power and of love and of a sound mind"* (2 Timothy 1:7) ... and *"Never again will I confess defeat, for God always causes me to triumph in Christ Jesus"* (2 Corinthians 2:14) ... and *"Never again will I confess worries and frustrations for I am casting all my cares upon Him Who cares for me"* (1 Peter 5:7); *in Christ, I am care-free!"* I quoted these affirmations daily. Soon I was hearing my own words, and was shocked at what I was hearing: "Never again will I fear?"

My life was radically transformed. My new positive words changed me from the inside out. My countenance changed: I walked taller, no longer had my head hanging low in defeat. After a few years, I remarried; I took this new way of living into this marriage, then into our children. I spoke these positive words into our children's lives daily as they jumped out of the car to go to school. I would say to them, "What kind of day are you going to have?" They would respond with, "A great day, because I can do all things through Christ Who strengthens me" (Philippians 4:13)!

Years passed, and I had an opportunity to go to Mexico City on a missions trip. I thought I was going to help build houses and serve the people there; but suddenly they whisked me to a crusade in an arena where there were 2,000 people assembled, worshipping the Lord. They told me I needed to preach to these people; they were waiting for me, with an interpreter. Although I didn't have much experience speaking to that many people, and there was a language barrier, still I nervously agreed to preach. I said, "Had I known this could have happened, I would have prepared something before coming to Mexico."

From the plane to the pulpit was about a 20-minute drive. I asked the Lord what I could possibly speak on ... when I realized I had Don's well-worn *"My Never Again List"* in my suit pocket. "Thank You, Lord!" I said – and that night, 2,000 people in Mexico City heard Don Gossett's *"My Never Again List,"* along with my own testimony. As Don had taught: *"God is no respecter of persons* (see Acts 10:34; also Romans 2:11); *what He did for me, He will do for you"* – now I had experienced it! Many came to the altar for prayer for their lives to be changed too.

I was ordained by Don Gossett in June 1995, and served as a board member for *Bold Bible Missions* for many years. My ministry, *Restoration Ministries*, began in 1995 and continues today. During twelve of those years, I was ministering in two federal prisons. Part of *Restoration Ministries* is a singing group, *Rhythms of Grace*, which includes myself, my wife Dorothy ... and Billy Bennett, the man who was my first wife's lover –

the man I had once plotted to kill. We three sing together and share our testimonies of God's faithfulness, forgiveness and restoration.

The power of one man, Don Gossett, to change thousands of lives! He had such an impact on me, on Dorothy, on our children and grandchildren, and the thousands of people we have touched in 20 years of *Restoration Ministries*. Even today, our daughter Kelly – who has been a surgical nurse for 15 years – stops, breathes, quotes *"I can do all things through Christ Who strengthens me"* before she faces a difficult task at work because she had that drilled into her from a young age (she is turning 36). Only Heaven will tell the impact of Don Gossett!

At a 1995 Board Meeting of *Bold Bible Missions* (back row, left to right): Judy Gossett ... Debbie McFadden ... Garth McFadden ... John Barker ... Dorothy Barker ... Eric Bidell ... Florence Eade ... Marisa Nyman ... Kenneth Halsey ... Jeanne Halsey; (seated) Don Gossett ... Debbie Gossett. (Photo provided by John and Dorothy Barker.)

- It is clear to us how great of a father you have had. A spiritual giant ... what a privilege to have been his children. ~ **Henry & Evonne Bierlink;** Lynden, Washington

- Another soldier has gone Home: *"Precious in the sight of the LORD is the death of His saints"* (Psalm 116:15). ~ **Cheryl Busse;** Saskatchewan
- We are so sorry to hear about your Dad. He sounds like an amazing man. We look forward to meeting him in Heaven. What a wonderful legacy he leaves here on Earth! ~ **Doug & Tracy Clark;** Custer, Washington

- How I love your family! Your father led so many to the Lord. He was one of the people who got me so excited about missions and sharing the Gospel. ~ **Dyan Colacurcio;** Rocklin, California

- He was a great man of God. His ministry has been a blessing for me. God bless you, and my prayers are with you. ~ **Paramjit Dari**

- What an amazing man he was. Thoughts and prayers, from Australia. ~ **Lesley Davis;** Brisbane, Queensland

## A Great Warrior of the Faith
### By **Rev. Michael R. Davis, Sr.**
Bellingham, Washington

I first met Uncle Don after I became engaged to his niece, Rita Rogers. Long before I moved to Washington and met my wife, my first

Nephew-in-law Michael Davis with Uncle Don Gossett. (May 18, 2014)

pastoral experience was in Florida, at *Trinity Christian International*. I was in charge of several church ministries there, and counseling was a part of my duties.

After we had become engaged, Rita first introduced me to Uncle Don; it was in the living room at my future mother-in-law's house. Rita had told me about the family relationship: Uncle Don was her uncle by marriage and her father's cousin – and she had told me that he was very influential in her upbringing. Of course, I knew him by name and reputation, but this was the first time of actually having the opportunity to sit down with him, one-on-one, to talk. With Uncle Don, all conversations would eventually turn to the subject of confessing God's Word and just the goodness of the Lord in general. I loved talking with him for that reason.

While we were talking, I mentioned my first pastoral experience in Florida, and told him that in counseling I (and the other staff) had always used a great list of positive confessions. I explained that I didn't know who had written it but it began with: *"Never again will I confess I can't...."* Uncle Don, always humble, just began to grin and kept on grinning as I told him how influential it had been in my own life and in other people's lives whom I had counseled, and how it had changed people's attitudes. He never said a word, just sat there smiling as I related all of this to him.

My then-fiancée (now my wife) was in the kitchen and heard some of the conversation. She walked into the living room and gently laid her hand on my shoulder, saying, "Honey, Uncle Don **wrote** the *Never Again List*!" I was dumbfounded for a second, and Uncle Don agreed, "Yes, that is right. I wrote it." He had sat there smiling, while I was talking, without saying a word about it. That is the truly humble man of God that he was. My wife and I have talked about it since, and I think he was enjoying the fact that his writing was impacting the lives of thousands, regardless of whether they knew who he was or not. Don Gossett, in my opinion, was a great warrior of the faith.

- Thinking of all the good times I shared with Don Gossett in New Zealand and traveling in India. Remember doing our confessions as we drove. I am so sad to hear Don passed away today. Glad to know he is gone Home. ~ **Charles Denton;** Federal Way, Washington

## The Key to Unlocking Destiny
By **Rev. Darcy Dubé**
*Kingdom Harvest Ministries International*
Delta, British Columbia

The first time I saw Don Gossett was incredible. He gave us all his little "to-do sheets" [*Bold Living Cards*]. Amazing! And books like *"How to Have Confidence"* ... *"The Gift of Praise"* ... *"The Praising Principle"* ... *"Praise Power"* ... *"Bible Answers For Today's Problems."* In many places I've been, I've taught the people of God about the power of praise, and *"What You Say Is What You Get"!*

So many times I saw him invite thousands of people to stand up, raise their right hands, take their left index fingers and tick off their right hands while saying, *"Praise the Lord!"* ten times. During our early ministry times, I'd often think, "Wow, during some of Don's biggest challenges, he understood that praise always brings the blessings of God!" Praise is the key to unlock your destiny.

Don Gossett was a man who unlocked one of God's greatest principles, an ageless promise that needs to transcend generations. What you saw is what you got with all of Don's life principles: simple but profound.

We lost a true warrior who knew how to release the presence of God through praise. *"Thanks, Don, for believing in us."* Don Gossett was our first apostle; he recognized our call, and encouraged Glenda and me to run the race God has put before us. Sometimes in life, we think, *"Did that person leave a legacy?"* Yes! It's a mark Don Gossett left in our hearts: to never give up, never give in, never look back, to never stop pursuing God's best. I will never forget the bountiful inheritance he left for us. Praise the Lord 10 times!

- I feel honored to have had Don believe in and recognize the call of God on our lives, and ordain us into full-time ministry. We spent many times with Don on his radio broadcast, sometimes going through the night during his "praise-a-thons." He always had a heart to let each of us speak the Word of God and pray for the sick. Over the years we had many experiences together; I even made Don a special 65th birthday for his celebration at *Vancouver Christian Centre*. Don did many services with us, and dedicated our youngest daughter to the Lord. My Mom and Dad loved him very much; and when my Dad passed away, we had Don come to do his service. Don has left a great legacy; I know in my life, if ever I am needing a breakthrough or a boost in my faith, I begin to "Praise the Lord" ten times! Blessings to all. ~ **Glenda Dubé;** Delta, British Columbia

- Blessed is Uncle Don, reunited with family and departed friends, in the presence of Jesus! ~ **Renée** (*née* Shackelford) **Dunning;** Baxter Springs, Kansas

- The entire Gossett family has blessed the Kingdom of God beyond measure! Judy introduced me to the *"Never Again" Confession,* and I still use it. ~ **Apostle Douglas L. Dye;** Douglasville, Georgia

- Don Gossett was a loved friend of Paul's and mine; we were honored to be called his friends. Paul often talked about the trip he and Don took together to attend a *Billy Graham Crusade*; it was a highlight of his life. We also had the privilege of attending the taping of Don's radio broadcast, being guests on his show. What an amazing servant of God! ~ **Kimberley Bannon Evinsky;** Guelph, Ontario

# Always A Big Part Of My Life
By **Jennifer** (*née* Halsey) **Freeman**
Blaine, Washington

Don Gossett with his first grandchild, Jennifer Halsey (daughter of Jeanne), the first "Office Baby." (1976)

I don't know anyone who loved a good "tribute" more than my grandfather did, so here goes. It's rare for a grandparent and grandchild to have the kind of relationship that we did, and I'm so grateful for that. I've been blessed that my Grandpa has always been such a big part of my life, both during my childhood and through my adult life as well.

We used to tease him about hanging up the phone without even saying goodbye when he was distracted or in a hurry. He didn't do that so much over the last few years; all our calls ended with, "I love you."

Grandpa was engaged in what was happening in my life to the very end. He was the kind of grandparent I will strive to be one day, and I see his influence in the way my parents interact with my kids. *"I will miss you and love you for always, Grandpa."*

Jen Freeman became CFO of *Bold Bible Missions* in 2002.

- Thinking of all your family. Your Dad used his special gifts for many years, and influenced so many, many people. He will be missed. ~ **Luella Forsythe;** Whitehorse, Yukon Territory

- So sorry for your loss. He was an amazing man! I believe and expect he is now experiencing great joy at his promotion to Glory. ~ **Mike French;** Lynden, Washington

Victoria *née* Gossett Froelich on her wedding day, with her grandfather; photo provided by Victoria Froelich. (April 12, 2002)

- Like my favorite photo of Grandpa and me from my wedding on April 14, 2012, I loved going in for a kiss and telling him how much I loved him. One day, I'll be able to tell him again. Until then, though my heart is heavy, I find peace in knowing that today, his heart is full as he praises his Lord whom he served so well! ~ **Victoria** (*née* Gossett) **Froelich;** Langley, British Columbia

- I am thinking about those *"Bank of Heaven Checks"* he had people write ... affirmations and promises from God! He gets to cash in his finally! ~ **Christine Karch Gilman;** Salem, Oregon

### Celebrating A Great Man
#### By **Brandon Gossett**

[AUTHOR'S NOTE: These are Brandon's remarks from his grandfather's Memorial Celebration.]

We are here to celebrate a great man. I am particularly here to give you all a glimpse of who he is as a grandfather. Or Grandpa. I can't really call him Don or anything else; doesn't feel right. He is the meaning of the word "Grandpa" to me. My wife and I birthed a little girl last year; we call *my* father – who is Don Gossett, Jr. – "Grandpa" ... but whenever anyone uses that title, I look for *my Grandpa,* Don Gossett, Sr. He is the definition of the word. And he earned it. Faithfully over his almost 40 years of grandfather-ness.

Brandon Gossett speaking at his grandfather's Memorial Service. (January 10, 2015)

As far as my assessment of my grandfather – I'll save the suspense: in private, my Grandpa was every bit as loving, faithful, sincere, generous, and upright as his public persona. And I would be in a good position to know this: we lived together for a time after my grandmother passed away in 1991. A very formative year for me ... probably the year in my life that shaped who I am as a man.

He taught me how to shoot a basketball ... how to write a book ... how to analyze a defense at high school basketball games. How to stay in touch with the people you love ... how to meet and engage people I don't know ... how to speak in front of people I don't know ... how to be an extrovert. How to love on my family ... how to be open-handed with resources ... how to be tender with those in suffering.

The education didn't stop when I was 9. You'll see photos of him with me later in life at basketball tournaments, at golf tournaments, at my college graduation in Denver, on the half court behind his office in Blaine, Washington, at my wedding. But his greatest "Grandpa feat" was calling me nearly every month for the past 12 years. I moved away for college in 2002 – he faithfully reached out to me at a predictable rhythm for the balance of that period.

The other grandkids and I, who loved him dearly, will remember:

- The several hundreds of fun lunches he sponsored.

- *"Silent Night"* on Christmas Eve, where he danced and sang/screamed what would normally be a very mellow song. His rendition of *"Silent Night"* was anything but calm but it *was* bright!

- *"Praising the Lord"* ten times at some of the most awkward times.

Speaking of awkward: we'd be out for lunch and he would love telling the waiter – who would be a complete stranger – all about his grandkids. As he would brag about me, I would be very embarrassed, thinking: *"Grandpa, they don't care! Let's allow this nice lady get back to work."* He'd offer these unsolicited summaries that "Jen is a straight A student" or "Samantha just got back from YWAM" or whatever.

It was very important to him that everyone knew I played college Golf in Colorado. The hostess would awkwardly try to escape without offending us as she slowly backed away from the table with a gracious smile.

Let's continue with the awkward. Surprise invitations to deliver a speech, or prayer, or testimony in front of an audience. If I really wanted to honor him right now, I would start to call out unsuspecting victims to the stage! My wife was not used to this, let me tell you. I thought this was normal behavior because I grew up sharing spontaneous testimonies ... and Grandpa made a point of not warning you so your message would be more authentic.

We all – save my cousin Alexander Halsey's family in India – got to be together at our cousin Jessica Nyman's wedding in October. The last time I saw him. A lovely wedding. My daughter on Grandpa's lap as she tried play with his fork ... talking about the *Seahawks* winning another Super Bowl ... the book he was working on ... and I can't recall the rest, but it was really good 30 minutes of one-on-one. I'll treasure that. I will miss him and his phone calls very much. *"Rest in peace, my sweet Grandpa."*

## Dad Was S.U.P.E.R.B.
### By **Michael Leon Gossett**

[AUTHOR'S NOTE: These are Michael's remarks from the Memorial Service.]

Michael Gossett's Ordination (left to right): his daughter Victoria Gossett ... his wife Shelley Gossett ... Michael ... his sister Jeanne Halsey ... his father Don Gossett. (2008)

My name is Michael Leon Gossett, and I am the first-born son of Donald Edward Gossett, Sr. I would like my daughter and son-in-law to stand, please. These people are Victoria and Justin Froelich, and this wonderful little baby is my first grandson Fraser Froelich. Fraser was born three days after my Dad went to be with Jesus. Our kids have honored my Dad by naming this little boy Fraser Robert **Edward** Froelich. "Edward" was, of course, my Dad's middle name. Thanks.

I want to say something about my Dad that you will remember, and the message is built around one word: SUPERB. The word "superb" describes my Dad very well. Not because he was perfect, but because he did so well with his 85 years of life and 65 years of ministry.

**S = Success.** Don Gossett came from nothing, and made a great success of his life. He worked hard, he studied, he kept at it. He had a vision, and he was passionate. He was called to preach, and he was constantly on the go. He had practical, memorial messages that transcended cultures. By any definition, Don Gossett was a success. Say it with me: *"**Don Gossett was a success.**"*

**U = Unique.** Don Gossett was a transplanted American to Canada. His formal education was limited, so he continually expanded his knowledge by studying, reading books and magazines, and meeting leaders all over the world. Rather than just repeat someone else's messages, Don Gossett faithfully preached the message that God gave him. Though he had hundreds of friends in ministry over 65 years, Don Gossett had a unique ministry. Say it with me: *"**Don Gossett was unique.**"*

**P = Purity.** Don Gossett mentored with some of the best-known ministries of the 1950s and he learned from them in two ways. He learned what to do and he learned what *not* to do. He saw the heavy price of sexual sin, and was successful in living out his 65 years of ministry by being pure. His candid message, *"Purity Is Power,"* was inspiring to many ministers all over the world. Say it with me: *"**Don Gossett practiced purity.**"*

**E = Encouragement.** Don Gossett was confident in his own callings, yet he loved to mentor and encourage other, younger ministers. He provided many opportunities for others to preach or testify, and to learn ministry in a hands-on way. Don Gossett wrote thousands of letters encouraging people to follow Jesus and serve Him whole-heartedly. Don Gossett had a habit of phoning many people every day and encouraging them, as well as praying for them.

Say it with me: *"Don Gossett was all about encouragement."*

**R = Realistic.** Don Gossett's spirituality was not designed for the ivory towers of seminaries, but rather for the daily street-level where ordinary people lived. On his radio programs, in his books and in his services, you didn't hear Don Gossett exploring the obscure portions of Revelations or the minor prophets. No, you heard him speak about living victoriously and serving the Lord ... about giving to others ... about having a vision for the whole world ... about receiving healing and direction ... about overcoming depression or bad habits ... about raising Godly children ... about being friendly and kind ... about being faithful in your job and marriage ... and about so much more. Say it with me: *"Don Gossett was very realistic."*

**B = Brief.** I could have said "bold" or "Biblical" but I chose "brief." Why? Because Dad believed in practical, accessible teaching. His *Bold Living Cards* are a perfect example of being brief yet effective. His *Power Poems* are another example, as are the *Bank of Heaven Prayer Checks*. Memorable, practical yet brief messages that stick with you. Don Gossett never bored you. There is a lot I could say about brevity but I can't ... because I want to be brief.

Let's stand to our feet, please. I have spoken briefly about Don Gossett's style of preaching. Now is your opportunity to participate with me in a little exercise that will help you remember something about Don Gossett's ministry: *"Come on, people, it's time to take a Praise Break. I want you to say 'Praise the Lord' with me and I want you to say it ten times. Now people, I don't want to hear any namby-pamby, half-hearted 'Praise the Lords' but rather a God-honoring, Devil-defeating declaration from your hearts. Are you ready? I said, 'Are you ready?' Praise the Lord! ... Praise the Lord! ... Praise the Lord! ... Praise the Lord! ... Praise the Lord! ... Praise the Lord! ... Praise the Lord! ... Praise the Lord! ... Praise the Lord! ... PRAISE THE LORD! Hallelujah!"*

## Standing on Grandpa's Shoulders
### By **Alexander Halsey**

Alex Halsey speaking at his grandfather's Memorial Service. (January 10, 2015)

A couple of people have asked to see the text of my Memorial speech that I gave for my grandfather, the one I got too choked up to finish.

While I also have a childhood full of fond memories and experiences with my grandfather, I'd like to focus on the ministry experiences we've shared, starting when I was a teenager. I had become a Christian when I was aged 5; then I committed my life to ministry in the summer of 1992, in the months before I started high school. My first opportunity to travel with Grandpa and his wife Debbie was three years later, when they invited me to join them to El Salvador; I was 17. These early trips really set the foundation for my thus-far 18 years in full time ministry.

This was my first time seeing my grandfather as a man of vision and faith, challenging people to accept Jesus and live out His Word. He was confident, powerful and authoritative, and knew the Word inside and out ... and wow, when I saw the crowds and the miracles, I realized that Grandpa was a big deal! *"He's really good at this! Who knew?"* I'm sure the personal pride I felt in my association with him wasn't entirely Godly, but this was my first taste the rich satisfaction that comes from changing lives in Jesus' Name.

My second trip was around a year later. This time I joined Grandpa and Debbie for three months in Australia and New Zealand. This was completely another side of his ministry: not quite so evangelistic, but more focused on building up and equipping the Body of Christ. This was also about fund-raising to support the great crusades in the developing world. This was the trip when I saw my grandfather as a man of humility, a man deeply dependent on God and in prayer. He'd carve out time to pray and praise before he'd take up the microphone.

Don Gossett conducting the Marriage Ceremony of his grandson Alex Halsey to Miss Cherry Beck; in Bangalore, Maharashtra, India. Alex's father Kenneth Halsey is seen standing as his Best Man. (July 13, 2002)

I realized he had a full second side to his ministry. He was funny and entertaining, yet he'd challenge people with simple and familiar Scriptures that we had somehow never applied to our daily lives. People loved him and were blessed by his sincere faith and endearing stories.

My final trip with them was to India, when I was 21 years old. India was bewildering, sweaty and unpredictable. This time, Grandpa was back in evangelism mode. His life of prayer and dependence on the Holy Spirit was up a couple notches, and God was undeniably using my grandfather, day in and day out. Miracles were frequent, and there was an atmosphere of faith and expectation I'd only read about in the book of Acts.

One of my tasks was to give an independent head-count of the big meetings. One series of meetings in Aizwal was so full of signs and wonders and the anointing of the Holy Spirit that the crowds grew from 1,500 the first night gradually up to 9,000 to 10,000 the final night. We spent four or five weeks traveling around India and something got inside of me. It might have been a parasite (smile), but that's when I began to dream about what it would be like to spend my life living among the people of India: *"Could I really live my life there happily, despite the great cultural differences?"* Now I've lived in India for twelve years, raising my family there with my Indian wife, equipping Indian pastors and apostolic leaders.

In addition to his first- and third-world ministries, there was a third major aspect to his ministry: that was mass communication through books and radio, and sometimes TV. These last few years – when my

A Four-Generation Family Walk (left to right): great-granddaughter Hayley Halsey (front of stroller) ... great-granddaughter Ava Freeman (back of stroller) ... grandson Alex Halsey (pushing stroller) ... great-granddaughter Aja Halsey, holding hands with granddaughter-in-law Cherry Halsey ... Don Gossett pushing great-grandson Jude Halsey on walker; in the far background are wife Debbie Gossett ... and son-in-law Kenneth Halsey. (2012)

family and I would be home on our annual visits – I'd make some radio broadcasts with him each time, and I was struck by how he was simultaneously professional (probably very few men have ever made more radio broadcasts in their lives) and how consistently prayerful and dependent on the Holy Spirit he was.

The foundation stones of my ministry and my life were set by the model of my grandfather: grounding all that I think and teach on the Word of God, living to bring Glory to the Name of Jesus. I'm so thankful for my heritage of faith and obedience, that I can stand on the shoulders of such a great man of God.

Recently my work in India has taken me out of the classroom and more into visiting our field locations in villages. When faced with prayer requests or health problems of these dear villagers in India, I often ask myself what would Jesus do ... but I also wonder, *"What would Grandpa do?"* I hope I can have an impact on both the next generation of my family and the next generation in India like my grandfather had on me and on India; helping them to be secure in their identity in Christ and to have an attitude of gratitude.

- It was an honor and privilege to work with your father. ~ **Greg Helgeth,** *COAST Physical Therapy*; Birch Bay, Washington

- Rejoicing with your Dad at his Home-going. Can't even begin to fathom the great multitude of witnesses because of his life, service and love. I'm so sorry for your loss, my friend. ~ **Tim Henderson,** Senior Pastor; *Jonathan Creek Christian Church*; Sullivan, Illinois

- All my love and prayers to the entire Gossett family. In loving memory of Don Gossett. Rest in Perfect Peace. ~ **Pattie Howard;** Beverly Hills, California

- In loving memory of Grandpa Don Gossett who ended his earthly journey at 3:30am. He will be dearly missed by his grandsons Brandon Gossett, Jordan Gossett and Justin Gossett, by all his family and grandchildren, and by countless others. As a Grandfather, he surpassed them all! ~ **Carrie Janzen;** Walnut Grove, British Columbia

## Author Don Gossett Leaves Legacy of Praise
By **Christine D. Johnson** ~ Posted 12 December 2014, *Charisma Online News*
Reprinted with permission

Robert Whitaker, Jr., publisher at Whitaker House Publishers, speaks at the Memorial Celebration. (January 15, 2015)

Best-selling *Whitaker House* author Don Gossett died Wednesday, December 10, 2014, at age 85; his wife Debra at his side, according to a ministry spokesperson. The prolific author was also a pastor, worldwide evangelist, missionary, and long-time broadcaster, serving in active ministry for 66 years.

Gossett was known for his teaching on praise and the power of the spoken word. Many of his books are considered classics, including *"What You Say Is What You Get," "There's Dynamite in Praise," "The Power of Your Words,"* and *"Words That Move Mountains,"* many co-authored with E.W. Kenyon. "We've lost a pioneer whose teaching impacted several generations," said *Whitaker House* President Bob Whitaker Jr. "Don Gossett was among the first to teach that ordinary people, not only the clergy, could stand on the authority of God's Word to teach, preach and heal in the name of Jesus."

Gossett began serving in ministry in the 1940s. He apprenticed with well-known evangelist T.L. Osborn, who encouraged him to launch his own evangelistic ministry. Gossett started his radio program, *"Bold Bible Living,"* in 1961. The broadcast grew to reach millions of listeners living in 89 nations.

His works have been translated into 18 languages, with more than 25-million copies distributed worldwide. "No matter how famous he became, Don was a gentleman with a humble and content spirit," Whitaker said. "He was a pleasure to work with and always an example of Jesus' love."

Gossett's legacy is guaranteed to live on with a new *Whitaker House* book co-authored by Kenyon and scheduled for release in 2015. Gossett's recent series of interviews on *"It's Supernatural!"* with Sid Roth are also available online at sidroth.org/television/tv-archives/don-gossett.

In recent years, Gossett had begun reaching a new generation via social media. Last year, after Osborn died, Gossett posted on Facebook what now serves as a fitting eulogy for himself: *"Precious in the sight of the Lord is the death of His saints. ... It was completely true that for him to live was Christ. Now he has received the 'gain' of Heaven."*

Don's first wife Joyce, with whom he had five children, died in 1991. He and Debra, an ordained minister, were married and have been partners in ministry since 1995. They planted a church in British Columbia, Canada — *Vancouver International Community Church*. They also have 11 grandchildren and eight great-grandchildren, and the ninth was born December 13 after Gossett passed.

A public "Home-going Celebration" to honor Gossett was held January 10, 2015.

- Your Dad was a gem and I enjoyed his kindness for me over decades. What a dear, compassionate man he was. He will be missed. ~ **Geri Karlstrom;** Surrey, British Columbia

- I am very sorry for the loss of your Dad but I rejoice with you that he is in Heaven with his dear Savior. ~ **Maggie Kinney;** Estes Park, Colorado

- So sorry to hear of your Dad's death — his graduation or promotion to Glory, actually. Will be praying for peace and a deep joy as you gather as a family to celebrate, reminisce and reconnect. ~ **Lando Klassen;** Abbotsford, British Columbia

- Don Gossett was such a wonderful man and a blessing to the world! ~ **Jeff Knight,** Senior Pastor, *Rock Church;* Monroe, Washington

- Already missing him so much. He impacted our lives across the globe too. He loved us and showed us his love. ~ **Konya Konyak;** Guwahati, India

- Sorry I will not be able to attend Don's funeral. He was a great man of faith and we had wonderful visits together over these many years. God bless and sustain you during this time. Your family is in our prayers. ~ **Rev. Billy Kroeze;** Everett, Washington

- I am so sorry to hear about your Dad. It was my honor to have been able to call him my friend. He was a funny guy! His greatest compliment was when he introduced me to his mother and told her I made an apple pie as good as hers. ~ **Lynda Langston;** Redding, California

- I am so sorry for your loss, but so grateful to God that Don is finally home with the One he told others about his entire life. We love you, and our prayers are with you at this time of grief and hope. ~ **Kurt Langstraat,** Senior Pastor, *North County Christ the King Community Church;* Lynden, Washington

- I'm sorry for your loss. I've never met a better man. I can't help but think of him entering the Gates of Heaven and being greeted by all the people whose lives he touched. ~ **Josh Lehman;** Phoenix, Arizona

## A Blessing To The Church and the World
### By **Pastor Lawrence Lim**
*New Creation Church;* Singapore

On behalf of **Pastor Joseph Prince** and *New Creation Church,* I would like to convey our deepest condolences to you and your family on the passing away of Brother Don Gossett. We pray for God to comfort and strengthen you during this time, and we declare the peace of God to guard your heart. Brother Don has been a blessing to the Body of Christ and to the world, and we have lost a man of God.

I still remember the times when he was in our church in Singapore; he has been a blessing to us. We will definitely miss him, and we are keeping you in our prayers during this time. God is with you; and if there is anything that you need, please let us know. Blessings!

- A piece of me left this Earth and lives in Heaven. Don was the only man who walked with me, shared his heart; a man with a mission. ~ **Peter Litchfield;** North Battlefield, Saskatchewan

## Your Father Impacted My Life
### By Wendy MacRitchie
Coquitlam, British Columbia

I have nothing but good memories of Don Gossett. From the time I was a little girl, my parents had nothing but wonderful things to say about your parents, especially your father. My dad always talked about how he gave your dad a winter coat when they first came to British Columbia; I personally think my dad was kind of proud of that!

He was always kind to me, very welcoming. As a very young teenager, I learned about God's promises: "Greater is He that is in me ... I can do all things through Christ ... I do not have the spirit of fear!" I loved working in the office at Blaine, with Judy; filling orders and having a chance to look at all the books he had written. It was a privilege and a blessing! When you heard of someone who was ill, it was natural to think of Rev. Gossett. Immediately I would be reminded of what I had learned, and put it into action. I learned how to greet people properly at his meetings.

These are sweet memories, Jeanne. I cherish the moment your father and I had at your house on July the 4th, when he cried about Judy. I felt so blessed that he felt comfortable enough with me to share his feelings. *"What you say is what you get"* – how many times have I said that! His influence is in my life; my beliefs, that you know that you know that you know! These are precious memories for me.

- What an amazing man full of grace and love. I am so grateful to have known him. ~ **Angie Farmer Mandjik;** Langley, British Columbia

- He was (and is!) a great man. ~ **Kimberly Martinson;** Lynden, Washington

- So glad I got to get a blessing and a personal word from your Dad at your *School of Creative Christian Writing.* ~ **Connie Matson;** Bellingham, Washington

## *My God Has Supplied All My Needs*
By **Rev. Garth McFadden**
Richmond, British Columbia

#2: NEVER AGAIN will I confess lack, for *"My God shall supply all my need according to His riches in glory by Christ Jesus."* (Philippians 4:19)

In 1984, in Ontario, Canada, I left my low-paying job at a local department store to start a career as a life insurance salesman. In

Garth McFadden speaking at the Memorial Celebration. (January 10, 2015)

my first year, at age 24, I broke the Rookie Record for Sales in my region. That year I earned $75,000 ... and did not look back for a number of years.

I lived a godless life of pushing for more success: big income, even bigger expenses. Between 1984 and 1988, I built two brand-new homes; the last one was built on a lot I had purchased on a street where I could build the biggest house around. When I drove home in the evening, I would cruise down my street really slowly in my top-of-the-line *Volvo* car, wearing my *Vaurent* sunglasses, so my neighbors could get a good look at what success was like. I was a husband and the father of three children ... and I was chasing something that was not real.

My life fell apart in June 1989, when I lost my father to cancer. In August 1989, my wife and I separated; eventually we divorced. I went from confident competitor to catastrophic collapse in a very short time. My big home filled with family was replaced with an empty, one-bedroom apartment. Within a few months, my bank called in my car loan and I was forced to sell it. My life insurance sales career became humiliating as I was forced to take the city bus to make my sales appointments. After the dust settled, all my assets were split and my home was sold, I was saddled with $40,000 of unsecured debt.

In the spring of 1990, God stepped into my life. I had literally been bribed by my sister with an airline ticket to fly to Vancouver, British Columbia, for the Easter weekend. The free ticket came with only one stipulation: that I go to her church with her husband

and herself. My first experience with Don Gossett's ministry came at his Good Friday High Noon service. That weekend, I dedicated my life to God.

My next trip to the West Coast came a few months later, at which time I experienced Don's ministry again. His confident use of the Word of God was inspiring. I bought his whole product line of books, cards and scrolls. As a bachelor back in Ontario, I was able to wallpaper my living room with Don's scrolls! The Word of God took on a new life for me.

The cornerstone of my daily affirmation was: *"NEVER AGAIN will I confess lack, for 'My God shall supply all my need according to His riches in glory by Christ Jesus.'"* I not only spoke it, but God made that Scripture come alive in me ... and I knew my debt was about to vanish.

Where has God brought me in the 25 years since that one-bedroom apartment and $40,000 of debt? I am completely debt-free! I have a beautiful home that is paid for, and we have savings in the bank. God has brought me a beautiful wife, and our family is restored. God has supplied all of my needs, and much more.

Over the years, Don and I developed a great friendship. He took me under his wing and mentored me in the ministry. He was my father in the faith. He taught me I was never more than a "praise break" away from being in the presence of God.

- We just heard of your Dad's passing, and our hearts go out to you. He had a great legacy that has been passed on to all his family and innumerable others. We were with a pastor from Zimbabwe last night who told us he had been so impacted by your Dad's books and tapes that, as a young boy, it led him into the ministry. Don will be greatly missed by many. ~ **Ray & Jo McLeod and Family;** White Rock, British Columbia

- I thank God for my precious friend Don Gossett. He was one of the very rare gems on Earth who blessed everyone he spoke to. ~ **Bjagu Moorjani**

- Prayers for your entire family. My Mom [his cousin Wanda] adored Don so much and spoke of him so often. ~ **Debi Moss;** Yuba City, California

- What a celebration he is having safely at Home in Heaven. Amazing legacy! Praise the Lord! ~ **Meredith Moyer;** Bellingham, Washington

- A good Daddy is so very hard to lose, no matter how old we "Daddy's girls" get. I am sorry for your loss; and pray the Celebration of his life is as sweet as he has been. ~ **Tina Nania;** Fairfax, Virginia

- I will miss Pastor Don Gossett. His life example, his books and CDs changed my life, especially *"The Power of Your Words"* and *"Purity Is Power"* books. He really helped me find identity in the faith; hearing his radio programs and meeting him in person was remarkable. He was very humble and helpful. God has a wonderful Eternal Reward for my beloved brother and friend. God bless him for everything; his legacy will live on. ~ **Shellan Naydew;** Burnaby, British Columbia

- Our thoughts and prayers are with your family. He touched so many lives and was a great man of God. May God bless you all. ~ **Ann Nelson;** Blaine, Washington

- What an incredible life he led! "Well done, My good and faithful servant." I can only imagine the conversation he is having this moment, catching up with Judy! So sorry for your loss, my dear sweet God-Aunt. ~ **Cynthia Hall Philpot;** South Beech, South Carolina

- Sorry to hear about Don's passing away. He certainly was one of the great men of God in modern church history. I was privileged to have some good talks with Don and hear of his many adventures in his journey of faith. I know he loved his family and I know you will all miss him. The world was a better place with Don here with us. But we all know his work is finished and now he cashes in on his great reward. God bless you all! ~ **Brian Pierson;** Abbotsford, British Columbia

## I Called Him "Padré"
### By **Reba Rambo-McGuire**

I had never seen anything like it: a family Bible study where people cracked jokes, segued from Holy Scripture to outrageous stories, and – Heaven forbid! – prayed with their eyes open while munching on corn

The "Other Sister" Reba Rambo-McGuire with her husband Dony McGuire.

chips. My ideas of such gatherings were primarily boring, religious and – come to think of it – almost non-existent. I mean, who really had family Bible studies with prayer in my hillbilly world? But somehow, all those years ago, I had landed in a different place up in Blaine, Washington. A world where families actually communicate from the heart and spoke their truth in love, often peppered with robust debate. For me, it was epic!

I can still see him sitting there: clad in that familiar dark suit, crisp white shirt and shiny dress *Florsheims* shoes on his firm-foundation feet. Larger than life, and fully engaged in the moment with his brood. Often amused, sometimes perplexed, yet allowing them this safe place for his children to speak their minds. Mama Joyce in her bright pink, tiny high-heels, kept a very close eye on me to see how I was faring in what was obviously a new experience for me. I had never met anyone like her either: bold, brassy, uninhibited, and totally free. I loved her instantly.

I was the stranger among them ... for about five minutes. Then somehow the line was crossed and there was an acceptance I had never quite known. Right there I understood my best friend Judy in a whole new way. I grasped the vine from which she grew, and I smiled with envy.

Don Gossett became "Padré" to me from that day forward. I'll never forget that first visit when we went walking 'neath his beloved full moon. I had read a couple of his books, and Jude has shared the essence of his teachings, but this just wasn't the same as experiencing the man and his amazing spirit. We journeyed through neighborhoods as I questioned him about the power of words. He turned a key in my mind and unlocked a whole new realm of understanding that has impacted my life to this day. He not only removed the scales from my eyes, but he unfurled my wings with the desire to soar upward into the very face of God. The revelations he imparted inspired, and were the rudder for many songs I've penned.

Judy Gossett was Reba Rambo's music producer for several years. (1978)

My soul is forever knit to Padré and all of the Gossett family. I send a sky-full of love and prayers to Debbie and all my family. I have had a lot of teachers but not many fathers. To me, Don Gossett will always be "Padré" = Father.

Here are two songs my husband Dony and I wrote after reading Padré's books: "*What You Say Is What You Get*" is because of what he taught us about watching our words to keep them aligned with God's

Word; and *"Never Again"* is my personal reminder to *"agree with God and disagree with the devil."* Both relied heavily on Judy's influence, in the composing and arranging.

### What You Say Is What You Get

(Chorus 1)  *Let the weak say, "I am strong"*
  *Let the sick say, "I am healed"*
  *With words of faith confess it*
  *And in the Name of Jesus, claim it*
  *What you say is what you get*

(Verse 1)  *Jesus said, "Whatsoever You shall ask*
  *In My Name, I will do it*
  *That the Father may be glorified in the Son"*
  *Joy and health, peace and forgiveness*
  *Strength to stand, life everlasting*
  *He has promised all these things*
  *To those He loves*

(Chorus 2)  *Let the blind say, "I can see"*
  *Let the lame say, "I can walk"*
  *With words of faith confess it*
  *And in the Name of Jesus, claim it*
  *What you say is what you get*

(Verse 2)  *You can choose life or death*
  *Every word you speak has power*
  *Just keep claiming every promise Jesus gives*
  *Don't give up, by faith believe it*
  *Stand your ground, you're going to see it*
  *Just reach on out and speak the Word and live*

(Chorus 3) *Let the deaf say, "I can hear"*
*Let the weary say, "I can rest"*
*Let the lost say, "I'm redeemed"*
*Let the troubled say, "I have peace"*
*With words of faith confess it*
*And in the Name of Jesus*
*Why don't you claim it*
*What you say, what you say*
*What you say is what you get.*

## Never Again

(verse 1) *Never again will I confess I can't*
*I can do all things through Christ which strengtheneth me*
*Never again will I confess worry (no!)*
*Casting all my cares on Him Who careth for me*

(chorus 1) *Never, never again, never, never again*
*Never again, no, never again, never again*
*I won't let me words defeat me, never again*

(bridge) *I'll possess what I confess*
*I am blessed with Heaven's best*
*Jesus is Lord, there is no room for my day to gloom*
*Never again, never again (never never, never never never again)*

(verse 2) *Never again will I confess sickness*
*With His stripes He took on His back*
*I know I'm healed*
*Never again will I confess defeat*
*Greater is He that's within me*
*Than who's in the world*

(chorus 2) *Never, never never again*
*Never, never never never again*
*Never again, no, never again*
*Never again*
*I won't let my words defeat me, never again*

(Ending) *No, never never never never again*
*Never never never never never again*
*Never again, no, never again*
*Never again*
*I won't let my words defeat me*
*I won't let my words defeat me*
*I won't let my words defeat me*
*Never again!*

- In year 1999, first time I had read book of Sir Don Gossett about saying positive Word of God in every situation that makes difference. It impact me so much in 2001, I had joined *Hindustan Bible Institute* in Madras to study Bible College; I have been given warning if I do not pay my college fees, I have to go home. It was hard situation. I use to continue speak positive Word of God which I learn, and I see miracle that in last moment some one came and paid entire my fees and did not reveal his name. Since that I got habit of speaking Word of God; as result, I have seen many doors open. I have taught my church members, and they too seen power of God in their situation. Thanks for Sir Don Gossett's life that impacted many lives in India. ~ **Sujit Shamuel Raut;** President, *Bridgestones Global Foundation,* Pune, Maharastra, India

- I feel so honored I was able to meet him at the *School of Creative Christian Writing*. He was a great man of God! ~ **Lorraine Robertson;** Lynden, Washington

- I'm really sorry to read about my dear cousin Rev. Don Gossett. Such a great man of God now is rejoicing with the others of our family in his Heavenly Home. Don has worked all of his life for this. He was so loved, and will be missed by so many. My thoughts, prayers and love goes to all of the family. ~ **Evelyn Rogers;** Redding, California

- Your father ministered and shared the Gospel with so many people. He was and will continue to be a great blessing, even though he's gone Home. ~ **Rosemary Reuss-Connors**

- He was a wonderful man and will be missed greatly. ~ **Jenn Ryan;** Lynden, Washington

- I'm so sorry, Gossett Family. You know my heart breaks for you; I'm trying to rejoice that another saint has finished his race (like we're supposed to) but right now, I'm sorry. Sending you all Big Hugs! We're here for you, as always. ~ **Danene Salomon Sepulveda;** Everett, Washington

- My Uncle Don Gossett went to his Eternal Reward this morning. In an era where so few finish well, he stayed the course to the end. He can truly say *"I have fought the good fight, I have finished the race, I have kept the faith."* Now he not only rests in peace but has endless joy at being reunited with his Savior and the host of saints, including a great number of family and friends, and has heard *"Well done, good and faithful servant. Enter into the joy of your Lord."* ~ **William L. "Bud" Shackelford, Jr.;** Baxter Springs, Kansas

- I'm so thankful he was my uncle; he will be missed. You are in our prayers. We love you. ~ **Angela Gregory Sherwood;** Salem, Oregon

- He will live in many people's lives, especially his famous *"Praise the Lord 10 times"*! ~ **Brenda Hoggard Smith-Elyk;** Coquitlam, British Columbia

## Don Gossett and His "Lacks"
By **David G. Spring**
Langley, British Columbia

I remember the first time I heard Don Gossett share his *MY NEVER AGAIN LIST*. It was at one of his Sunday afternoon meetings in Vancouver, B.C. I was asked to help hand out the cards to those in attendance.

Often Don would – with a very brief introduction – launch into the recitation of the card he was sharing at the meeting, but this time was different. Don shared the story of how this *MY NEVER AGAIN LIST* came into being and how it had changed his whole walk with God from that time forward.

He told us of a successful ministry trip to Victoria, British Columbia – successful ministry, but not successful in what seemed most important to him at that time. There was rent to pay when he got home, but it seemed the giving had not been what was needed to cover the bills waiting at home. It became a time for reflection, and maybe a time to consider the call of God on his life. *"Would God call him and send him out, but not meet his needs?"*

Don then shared about talking to God about the apparent lacks in his life. Was God unable to support him? This was the time when the Lord started to remind him that instead of speaking the Word of God, he was speaking his circumstances: his lacks, his needs. Don then realized that the only way to turn this around was to start to speak the Word of God rather than what was in front of him.

Don then shared how this became a turning point in his life. Never again would he let circumstances replace the Word of God. After sharing about this turning point and how God had begun to lead him to those verses, it was now time to read this card together out loud.

We did that – and yes, I could see the value in every point. Every one of the twelve affirmations would make us stronger, but the important question was: *"Did I take that card home and read it aloud every day?"* No. I have to say I failed in the task, but I believe I did receive something very important that day. I may not have realized it right away, but later I could see that I caught the essence of what Don Gossett's *MY NEVER AGAIN LIST* was all about.

My confession in the circumstances which confronted me in the days to come were met with the Word of God. I understood that my peace and my success were rooted in the positive confession. From Don Gossett I learned that never again would I let anything which confronted me lift itself above the Word of God. I would be that overcomer!

*"Thank you, Don Gossett!"* He was a great friend, and I will miss him.

- He was an amazing man of God, such a comfort to grow up around. ~ **Sasha Stanfill;** Blaine, Washington

- He will be missed so much by all who knew him. ~ **Lois Lea Starrett;** British Columbia

- Your Dad was a wonderful man who stood for purity. Bless you. ~ **Elizabeth Storbo;** New Westminster, British Columbia

- What an amazing legacy, thousands of lives he has touched. He will be remembered! ~ **Becki Taylor;** Bellingham, Washington

- He fought a good fight and now is Home with his Lord. Praying for all of you. ~ **Jo Anne Tell;** Bellingham, Washington

- Your Dad was such an amazing spiritual father to many, including me. I know you will miss him immensely as he will be greatly missed in the Body of Christ. I know he is rejoicing in the presence of Jesus! ~ **John E. Tracy**

- Don Gossett impacted most people with his preachings, but he impacted my life with his kindness and patience. He gave me my first job working in an office; I think I was 14 or 15. With way more chances than I deserved, he helped me develop my office skills which ultimately influenced the direction of my career. I am so grateful for this. ~ **Barbara Trainer;** Langley, British Columbia

- Don Gossett was a man of the Word and of faith. Wendy and I were young and just getting into ministry when Don inspired me to believe and to speak the Word of God. Now, 35 years later, we realize how valuable his lessons were. His spirit and faith will continue to impact our world through generations to come. ~ **Casey Treat,** Senior Pastor; *Christian Faith Center;* Federal Way, Washington

- Sorry to hear this. Your father was an awesome man! Praying for you and your family during this time. ~ **Laurie Jensen Vervaecke;** Sandy, Utah

- Tears of sorrow and joy. He impacted many lives. May your family share in the rest-assured peace of Christ Jesus today. Don Gossett was a great man of God and will never be forgotten! He raised an amazing and strong God-guided family whom we have grown to love so much as if we were part of them! He is now in a better place and probably singing with that choir Aunty Judy has up there. And we know he has said those famous Don words:

*"Praise the Lord ten times!"* ~ **Arie & Steve Waymen;** Calgary, Alberta

## Not Easily Forgotten
By **Pastor Dennis White**
Brampton, Ontario

I first met Don Gossett back in the mid-1960s, when my wife and I served in Christian ministry on the island of Dominica, in the Caribbean. From that time to 2007, Don ministered to our congregations in Dominica ... St. Vincent ... Trinidad and Tobago ... Bermuda ... Nairobi, Kenya, East Africa ... and in Mississauga, Ontario, Canada.

Don's love and appreciation for the Word of God, and his vibrant declaration of its truths from pulpits, crude crusade platforms and radio stations have, without doubt, helped to extend the Kingdom of our Lord worldwide. Don's flare for communicating the Word of God in a simple, readable style made his books popular in many Third World countries.

As a friend, Don's big heart, his love for wife and family, and his enormous appetite for extending the out read of the *Bold Bible Living* ministry are things not easily forgotten. My wife Esther and I extend to Debra and the entire Gossett clan our deepest condolences, and pray that the sufficiency of God's grace will keep you in this hour, and equip you to uphold the legacy he has left you.

- I have nothing but very fond memories of your Dad. I remember going to his house and the offices way back. Despite your Dad's many travels and global ministry, he was very down to Earth, so positive and warm. In recent years, each time he saw me he eagerly asked what I was up to, wanted to know about all my vocational changes. He exuded care and sincerity, and prayed for me with fervency on many occasions, for guidance on the road ahead. Last time I saw him, same thing; he really meant it and listened intently. A great man inspires others to want to be better – your Dad exemplified that. ~ **Jeremy Wiebe;** Langley, British Columbia

- I had the privilege of working for your Dad for two years, and he was indeed a wonderful man of God. He was certainly a *"faithful servant"* and now will spend Eternity with the One he served. ~ **Shirley** (*née* Halsey) **Wiebe;** Walnut Grove, British Columbia

- As young believers and then as pastors, your Dad's ministry, teachings and example as a Godly man impacted our lives. You are a blessed family. ~ **Pastors Warren & Patricia Willie;** Muncie, Indiana

# AFTERWORDS

# EULOGY
## Written by **Jeanne Halsey**
## ~ Delivered by **Kenneth** and **Jeanne Halsey**

Many people know about the essential details of the life of Don Gossett –

- how he was born in Oklahoma during the Great Depression, proud of his Cherokee heritage;
- how he was raised in an impoverished, non-Christian family, with an alcoholic, often abusive father;
- and despite his God-less upbringing, how Don came to faith in Christ at the age of 12;
- of his call to full-time ministry at age 19, despite having a strong speech impediment;
- and of his wife Joyce and their five children Michael, Judy, Jeanne, Donnie, and Marisa

– but those are "details" that don't explain the "why and how" God transformed him from a shy young man into a powerful preacher of the Gospel.  *Here* are those reasons.

### Student of God's Word

In his teens, Don Gossett became a man who avidly studied God's Word.  He memorized great portions of the Bible; you could ask him, "Don, where does the Bible talk about 'a pure heart'" ...

and instantly he would be quoting Psalm 24:4, *"He that hath clean hands and a pure heart, who hath not lifted up his soul unto vanity nor sworn deceitfully."* Of course, Don always used King James.

His was a simple faith; he believed the Bible meant exactly what it said, he accepted the promises of God as available for today, and he always turned the focus back to God through praise and thanksgiving. His absolute trust in God's Word was the main thing that defined him throughout his life.

**Prayer and Faith**

Don believed in the power of prayer. An example of his faith meeting with prayer was in August 1953, when his wife Joyce became very ill with Rheumatic Fever after the difficult birth of their third child, Jeanne Michele. For the next eight months, Joyce was totally bedfast, her body swollen and in great pain, unable to care for herself or the three little babies. Don came off the field of evangelism to care for his invalid wife and their young family, briefly taking a job as a Bible salesman.

On Easter Sunday 1954, Don was reading the Word aloud to Joyce; when he read Psalm 27, the first verse – *"The LORD is my light and my salvation; whom shall I fear? The LORD is the strength of my life; of whom shall I be afraid?"* – this is when the phrase *"the LORD is the strength of my life"* suddenly came alive ... and Joyce rose up from the bed proclaiming this promise from God's own Word. Slowly at first and then with increasing strength, Don and Joyce walked through their little house, declaring God's Word with each step ... and Joyce was soon completely healed.

Don and his family drove their 1956 Buick all over the United States and much of Canada, and he imparted his love for God's Word into their children. Traveling for long hours, he would drill the kids in memorizing Bible verses and building a rich heritage of trusting God in all things into their lives. Never was a car-trip started without him praying, *"Dear Lord Jesus: Keep us from harm and danger, disease and affliction. Amen!"* The family knew they were safe when Daddy prayed.

### Growing in Faith

Don's habit of deeply studying the Bible was the key to another tremendous change in his life. In 1960, Don had moved his family to Victoria, British Columbia, where he was endeavoring to support them as a traveling evangelist, speaking in little churches up and down the west coast of the United States, all over Vancouver Island, throughout British Columbia and into the Interior. It was an arduous struggle for Don, especially leaving his family at the little motel for days at a time, and their financial prospects were very dim.

In a season of desperate prayer, he faced his own fears – fear of financial lack, fear of failure, fear of illness, and so on – and God answered him through His Word, giving Don a "heart transplant" that would radically change his whole ministry. On the flyleaf of his Bible Don wrote out the teaching that would become one of his most popular messages: *"MY NEVER AGAIN LIST."* These truths are popularly known, but heart it again carefully to catch Don's own heart about those situations in his own life which motivated each phrase.

Through these original twelve affirmations, you clearly see the young Don Gossett, a man growing into his faith and ministry through his own trials and tribulations, who wrote them down and then shared them with the world, to bring great glory to God!

## The Practice of Praise

From *"fighting the good fight of faith,"* leaning strongly on God's Word, Don began the next step: he developed "the attitude of gratitude" by learning to practice praise:

*A good man out of the good treasure of his heart brings forth that which is good; and an evil man out of the evil treasure of his heart brings forth that which is evil; for out of the abundance of the heart his mouth speaks.*
**Luke 6:24**

*But You are holy, O Thou Who inhabits the praises of Israel. Our fathers trust in You; they trusted, and You delivered them. They cried unto You, and were delivered; they trusted in You, and were not confounded. ... He trusted on the LORD that He would deliver him; let Him deliver him, seeing he delighted in Him.*
**Psalm 22:3-5,8**

Don Gossett was a man whose heart was abundantly filled with praise to God for His goodness – for all the answers to prayer, the opening doors of opportunity, the supernatural healings He poured through Don's ministry – so that he was compelled to research "praise" in the Bible ... and came up with a whole new teaching that focused on God's people giving Him glory! His children Judy and Donnie wrote a song, *"God Inhabits the Praise of His People,"* which was used for years as the theme of his radio broadcast. Don became known as the "Praise-Walking Man," renowned for his *"Praise the Lord ten times."* He published *"Praise Power"* ... *"The School of Praise"* ... *"Praise Avenue"* ... *"Praise Walk"* ... and many other titles that empowered people to understand the great spiritual power in praise. Don Moen's *"Give Thanks"* became one of the longest-running themes on the *Bold Bible Living* radio program.

## Willingness and Sense of Adventure

Another aspect that defined Don Gossett was his sense of adventure and willingness to take the Gospel to the world. At first he focused on the West Indies, but in 1974, when *Whitaker House Publisher* picked up his books, translated them into 32 languages and distributed them globally, Don began receiving invitations to preach around the world. So often when he arrived overseas – in China, in Russia, in Africa, in Australia, in South America, in India, in 50-plus nations to where he traveled for ministry – he would find tattered, much-circulated, even photocopied copies of his books, which enabled him to reach into the lives of peoples of other nations with the truths of God's Word that he had proven in his own life.

One of these people was a young man in Singapore, the son of mixed-faith parents who had raised their son as an agnostic. He saw *"The Power of Your Words"* in the window display of an occult book store and thought, "I could use some power in my life," so he went inside and bought the book. He read it through twice ... and gave his heart to Christ, then endeavored to contact the book's author in North America. This young man asked Don to become his "spiritual father," and through Don's mentoring, Joseph Prince rose up to become a hugely-fruitful Charismatic pastor in Singapore and preacher around the world. Don's books were bearing tremendous fruit.

Overseas travel loses it's "exotic luxury" aspect very quickly. Climate changes, difficult travel schedules, different foods, language barriers, the many contrasts between North America and the third-world nations – none of these deterred Don Gossett from fulfilling a statement he learned from John Keith Falconer and adopted as his own early on: *"If I have but one candle, let me burn it out in a land flooded with darkness than in a land flooded with light."* He developed a heart for the nations, and was always willing to subject his body to travel rigors in order to reach that special moment when he stepped up to the microphone to preach the Word of God, hearing it translated into many languages, and then stretching out his hands to tirelessly pray for the sick.  He believed in *"If Nobody Reaches, Nobody Gets Touched"* and actively practiced *"To win a soul is my goal,"* even if it was simply talking to the driver of the taxi-cab and leading him to Christ.

Don's was the now-old-fashioned mass-evangelism style he had seen in his teens and twenties, when traveling with Jack Coe, W.W. Freeman and T.L. Osborn, and his ministry would attract "scores of thousands" (one of his favorite phrases) in open-air meetings.  He saw miraculous healings from life-threatening diseases – saw cataracts melt from people's eyes, "proved" the healing of people who were deaf in one or both ears with his famous "retreating *'Hallelujah,' 'Praise the Lord,' 'Glory to God,' 'Philadelphia'*" phrases," saw miracles of healing from AIDS, witnessed demons cast out, watched impossible illnesses reversed to wholeness ... and so much more – and he personally led well over one-million people in praying the Sinner's Prayer for Salvation.  Don Gossett was known for preaching with a tender smile on his face and great joy in his voice. He truly was in his element when ministering overseas.

## Generosity and Compassion

Another strong characteristic of Don Gossett was his innate generosity. Perhaps because of growing up in poverty and enduring rejection in his early years of ministry, Don had a compassionate heart as a generous father, friend and fellow minister. He helped launch ministries of "newcomers" like Benny Hinn, Joseph Prince, Roscoe Ronnie Jessie Coyne, to name a few — and opened new opportunities for "old-timers" like Betty Baxter, William Caldwell, Max Solbrekken, among others. Then there was this young pastor's son from California who was working with *Teen Challenge's Addicts Choir*, whom Don brought up to Vancouver for a series of concerts — he was in his 20s and his name was Andraé Crouch. In later years, Don's children was the opening act for Andraé Crouch and the Disciples at a Youth Conference in Hawaii; the Crouches became close family friends, and daughter Judy worked as Road Manager for

Don's eldest daughter Judy A. Gossett (1952-2003), with long-time family friends, twins Sandra Crouch and Andraé Crouch (1942-2015; who died one month after Don). (1995)

Andraé Crouch and the Disciples (and was Maid of Honor at Sandra's Crouch's wedding).

Don's generosity and compassion motivated him to buy musical instruments for budding singers, sponsored overseas travel for fledgling evangelists, shared his radio time with ministries of every stripe.  He was one of the few who fellowshipped with Jim Bakker after his release from prison.  He practiced forgiveness and restoration, shared of his finances, his wisdom, his guidance, his attention and time.  He took his kids to *Disneyland* several times!  He often said, *"Only one life, will soon be past / Only what's done for Christ will last."*  He poured out of his own means to bless others in need, he *"laid up treasures in Heaven"* and he actually left very little behind beyond his own legacy.

He counted among his very close fellow ministers strong men like Rev. Dennis White from Trinidad ... Dr. John Lucas of Calgary ... the late Rev. Holmes Williams of Barbados ... the late Pastor Paul Olson of Minneapolis ... Rev. Alan Davies of Australia ... Brother Dhinakarin from India ... Pastor Scott Stanek from Texas, and so many others – people of integrity, vision, boldness, and Godliness.

## Setbacks

Three distinct setbacks in Don's later life had significant impacts. First was when his beloved wife Joyce suffered years of heart disease and finally succumbed in 1991, dying at age 62; they had been married 41 years.

But God had a plan in the works for Don's good: on Vancouver Island there was a sweet woman who had decided to refrain from dating or marriage until God brought His chosen man into her life. She had heard Don Gossett preach on the radio, and was especially drawn to his message on the power of the blood of Jesus, but she had not met him.

After Joyce's death, Don needed a ministry companion, someone with a Biblical worldview and a desire to reach the nations for Christ – and Debra Gail Deane had been willing to wait for God's perfect partner and plan for her life. Don had come to minister at her local church in Victoria, where she was an

Don and his second wife, Debra Gail (*née* Deane) Gossett. (May 13, 2005)

associate pastor.  Rev. Gossett met Miss Deane … and in 1995, he married this wonderful woman whom God had chosen for him.  At that time, Debbie immediately inherited two step-sons, three step-daughters, two step-daughters-in-law, two step-sons-in-law, eleven step-grandchildren, and one step-great-grandson – and she became known as "Marmee" to her new family.

The first decade of their marriage, Don and Debbie Gossett traveled extensively around the world, ministering together in many nations, in many unusual circumstances, with wonderful responses to salvation and outstanding miracles of healing.  Debbie learned quickly, first-hand, the rigors and the rewards of overseas' travel and ministry; and she indeed was his God-given partner in marriage and evangelism.  What was a setback turned to a great gain!

Then another setback occurred when Don's eldest daughter, the effervescent Judy Gossett – a renowned singer, songwriter, musician, arranger, record producer, and pastor of *The River at Vancouver* – died suddenly from previously undiagnosed cancer in 2003.  This was the unexpected blow which led to Don's major heart attack six months later while he was ministering in Barbados.  Over the next eleven years, Don's health gradually but steadily declined, and his traveling days were over.

## His Legacy

Undaunted by ill health, Don continued to make radio broadcasts and to write books, and he participated with Debbie in the church they established in Vancouver, *International Community Church.* He took great joy in writing partner letters and staying in touch with the thousands of people who shared in his 65 years of ministry. He was exceedingly proud of his grandson Alexander Halsey – son of his daughter Jeanne and her husband Kenneth Halsey – because Alex had traveled extensively with his grandfather and step-grandmother on missions trips to Central America, Australia and New Zealand, and to India. In 2002, when Alex married Miss Cherry Ruth Beck, a native of India, Don performed the wedding ceremony in Bangalore. Today Alex – who once suffered from a speech impediment like his grandfather – lives in India full-time, and administrates the *Biblical Academy* of the *Life-Giving Network,* which is training indigent pastors in church-planting all over that nation. India held a special place in Don's heart, so for his grandson to be continuing in ministry in that nation was very important to him.

Don Gossett with some of the ladies in his life (back row, left to right): granddaughter Rebekah Nyman ... wife Debbie Gossett ... great-grandson Jack Pedersen ... granddaughter Vanessa Pedersen ... granddaughter Jessica Nyman ... daughter Jeanne Halsey; (front row) granddaughter Samantha Nyman ... Don. (Summer 2013)

As we are here today, Don's granddaughter Rebekah Nyman – daughter of his daughter Marisa and her husband Ken Nyman – is in Guatemala, Central America, on the outreach portion of *Youth With A Mission's* "Discipleship Training School." At various times, all five of his children have been active in full-time ministry, and many of his grandchildren – and even his nephews and nieces – have stepped out in faith in ministry. Don's heart for the nations has truly been planted into the hearts of his offspring, several whom have ministered with him both in North America and overseas. This is the inheritance they have from their patriarch:

> *"Ask of Me, and I shall give thee the heathen for thine inheritance, and the uttermost parts of the Earth for thy possession."*
>
> **Psalm 2:8**; NLT

When Don's eldest great-grandson Kristian Freeman — son of Don's granddaughter Jennifer and her husband Patrick Freeman — was very young, he tried to say *"Grandpa Gossett"* but it came out as *"Grandpa God."* This is how he became known by his many of eleven grandchildren and nine great-grand-children, each of whom was a great blessing to him. Just the other day, Kristian's sister, 9-year-old Ava, was saying, *"I always felt so comfortable with Grandpa God because he was so close to God. When I was with him, I knew I was with God too."* Don Gossett was a very real man, a big-hearted loving husband, father, grandfather, and great-grandfather, much beloved by his family, and he modeled the Heavenly Father's heart to them.

A man of God's Word ... a man of prayer and faith ... a man of praise and joy ... a man of compassion and generosity ... a willing adventurer — these were the God-elements that shaped Donald Edward Gossett (senior) for his whole life, which enabled him to have a deep impact on the nations. Now he has experienced that life-long goal, where he has knelt at the Throne of God and heard Him say: *"Well, Don? Well done!"*

*"Well done, My son, My good and faithful servant. You have been faithful over what I gave you, so now I will make you fruitful*

*over many things. Enter into the joy of your Lord and into your eternal reward!"*
**Matthew 25:21**; paraphrased

To the end of his days, Don Gossett was a man of God who practiced this verse diligently –

*Let us hold tightly without wavering to the hope we affirm, for God can be trusted to keep His promise.*
**Hebrews 10:23**; NLT

– and he has received his great reward!

**The Rev. Dr. Donald Edward Gossett, Senior**
July 20, 1929 ~ December 10, 2014

# OBITUARY

## DONALD EDWARD GOSSETT
July 20, 1929 ~ December 10, 2014

**Rev. Dr. Donald Edward Gossett** (Sr.), 85, has died after a brief illness. At 19, Rev. Gossett entered Christian ministry and was active until his death; daily programs on Radio KARI and other stations continue. He published over 200 books, with *"What You Say Is What You Get"* his multi-million bestseller (translated into 32 languages and distributed internationally); his publisher releases another book in 2015.

Don Gossett was born at home in Anadarko, Oklahoma, U.S.A.; he experienced *"the happiest day of a Christian's life"* at St. Joseph's PeaceHealth Hospital in Bellingham, Washington. Rev. Gossett was preceded in death by his first wife **Joyce Aletha** (*née* Shackelford) **Gossett** (1929-1991); by his daughter **Judith Anne Gossett** (1952-2003); by his parents **Robert Edward Gossett** and **Lillie Jane Gossett**; by his sister

Don and Joyce Gossett on their 40th Wedding Anniversary. (January 10, 1990)

**Donnis Oneida** (*née* Gossett) **Thomas** and brother-in-law **Delbert Thomas**; and by his brother his **Richard Leon Gossett**.

Don and his second wife, Debbie. (2009)

Rev. Gossett is survived by his second wife **Debra** (*née* Deane) **Gossett**; his son **Michael Leon Gossett** [and daughter-in-law **Shelley J. Gossett**; and granddaughter **Victoria Jane Froelich,** grandson-in-law **Justin Froelich**, and great-grandson **Fraser Robert Edward Froelich** (who was born 3 days after Don died), and grandson **James Gossett**]; his daughter **Jeanne Michele** (*née* Gossett) **Halsey** [and son-in-law **R. Kenneth A.J. Halsey**; and granddaughter **Jennifer Elisabeth Joy** (*née* Halsey) **Freeman** (and grandson-in-law **Patrick M. Freeman**, and great-grandson **Kristian Michael Alexander Freeman** and great-granddaughter **Ava Michelle Freeman**), and grandson **Alexander John Edward Halsey,** (and granddaughter-in-law **Cherry Ruth** (*née* Beck) **Halsey,** and great-grandson **Jude Alexander Halsey**, and great-granddaughters **Aja Amara Halsey** and **Hayley Anne Halsey**]; his son **Donald Edward Gossett,**

Junior [and grandson **Brandon Gossett,** (and granddaughter-in-law **Kelsey Gossett,** and great-granddaughter **Piper Joy Gossett**); and grandsons **Jordan Gossett** and **Justin Gossett**]; and his daughter **Marisa Lynnette** (née Gossett) **Nyman,** [and son-in-law **Ken R. Nyman;** and granddaughter **Vanessa Kathryn** (née Nyman) **Pedersen** (and grandson-in-law **Jared Pedersen,** and great-grandson **Jack Jared Pedersen** and great-granddaughter **Grace Kathryn Pedersen**); granddaughter **Jessica Ariel** (née Nyman) **Collier** (and grandson-in-law **Jordan Collier**); and granddaughters **Rebekah Diana Michele Nyman** and **Samantha Marisa Nyman**]; and numerous nieces and nephews.

At the grave side (left to right): former daughter-in-law Carrie Janzen ... grandson Justin Gossett ... granddaughter Samantha Nyman ... son-in-law Ken Nyman ... daughter Marisa Nyman ... widow Debbie Gossett ... (facing away from camera) great-granddaughter Ava Freeman ... daughter Jeanne Halsey ... (head bowed, behind) grandson-in-law Jordan Collier. (December 15, 2014)

A private family Funeral was held Monday 15 December 2014, at *Peace Arch Assembly Church* in Blaine, Washington, with Interment at the *Enterprise Cemetery* in Ferndale, Washington. A public Memorial was held on 10 January 2015, at *First Baptist Church* in Vancouver, British Columbia. In lieu of flowers, donations may be given to the **Don Gossett Memorial Fund,** at **www.dongossett.com**.

The last-known photo of Don Gossett, taken December 1, 2014; with his great-granddaughter Grace Kathryn Pedersen, at his home in Blaine, Washington.

# DEDICATION

This book about our father is dedicated to my three siblings: to my older brother **Michael Leon Gossett** ... to my younger brother **Donald Edward Gossett, Junior** ... and to my younger (remaining) sister **Marisa Lynnette (*née* Gossett) Nyman.** He was our father; we lived MY NEVER AGAIN LIST with him. This is our heritage; we are his treasures, and will carry on his good name. Let us each purpose to continue to live our lives as *"bold as a lion"* (see Proverbs 28:1)!

**The Gossett Family in 1967 at the "Miracle House" in Surrey** (back row, left to right): Donnie ... Michael; (front row): Marisa ... Jeanne ... Don (1929-2014) ... Joyce (1929-1991) ... Judy (1952-2003).

## ABOUT THE AUTHOR

Jeanne Gossett Halsey and her husband Kenneth Halsey, at the Memorial Service for her father Don Gossett. (January 10, 2015)

Jeanne Michele (*née* Gossett) Halsey is a daughter, sister, wife, mother, grandmother, cousin, aunt ... and a writer. Third of five children born to international missionary-evangelist Dr. Don E. Gossett and his wife Joyce Shackelford Gossett, Jeanne naturally inherited her father's gift of writing (he published over 120 books, including the best-selling *"What You Say Is What You Get"*). Jeanne was born in Oklahoma ... immigrated to Canada at age 7 ... was educated in British Columbia (*Douglas Junior College, the University of British Columbia*) ... and has resided in Oklahoma, Oregon, British Columbia, Washington state, Texas, and Colorado. She has traveled extensively internationally.

Formerly Managing Editor of two internationally-distributed monthly Christian magazines, Jeanne is a freelance writer. She has ghostwritten and published books for several renowned Christian ministries and contemporary personalities: for her father ... Reinhard Bonnke ...

Sarah Bowling ... U. Gary Charlwood ... Frank Colacurcio ... Marilyn Hickey ... Kurt Langstraat ... Danny Ost ... Paul Overstreet ... Kim Ryan ... Cliff Self ... Robert Tilton ... Steve Scroggins ... Steve Watt ... and many others.  She has written for Christian and secular trade and online magazines, and has published several Sports articles about *National Basketball Association* superstar Luke Ridnour for *Sports Spectrum* Magazine (a division of *Christianity Today*).  She has published an Internet newsletter *e-Jeanne,* and frequently teaches *The School of Creative Christian Writing*, using her book *"The Legacy of Writing"* as the curriculum.

    Jeanne lives in Birch Bay, Washington, with her husband (since 1974) Kenneth Halsey, *Vice President of Franchise Sales,* Western Region, for *The Realogy Corporation;* their empty-nest home includes two purebred Chihuahuas, Lucia Gracias Royale and Juliet Diva Royale.  Their daughter Jennifer is married to Patrick Freeman; they have two children, Kristian and Ava; and thankfully the Freemans live very nearby, in Blaine, Washington.  Their son Alexander is married to Cherry Ruth; they have three children, Jude, Aja and Hayley; the younger Halseys live halfway around the world, stationed in Ranchi, Jharkhand, India, as full-time missionaries with *The Life-Giving*

*Network*, an outreach of *North County Christ the King*.

An outspoken activist for Christian causes, Jeanne has stood for public office. She is past-Chair of the Board of Directors of the *Whatcom County Pregnancy Clinic*, and is past-Secretary of the Board of Directors of the *Greens at Loomis Trail Homeowners Association*. Jeanne and Kenneth are active members of *North County*

**Jeanne Halsey's Family** (back row, left to right): son-in-law Patrick Freeman ... husband Kenneth Halsey ... Jeanne ... grandson Kristian Freeman ... niece-in-law Kelsey Gossett ... son Alexander Halsey; (front row) granddaughter Ava Freeman ... granddaughter Aja Halsey ... grandson Jude Halsey ... daughter-in-law Cherry Halsey ... granddaughter Hayley Halsey (in front) ... daughter Jennifer Freeman ... nephew Brandon Gossett. (2003)

*Christ the King Community Church* in Lynden, Washington. Her signature Scripture:

> *Let your light shine before men that they can see your good works and glorify your Father Who is in Heaven.*
> **Matthew 5:16**; NLT

# OTHER TITLES BY JEANNE HALSEY
*All titles can be purchased directly from www.Lulu.com or from www.Amazon.com*

## Non-Fiction

**BEHOLD THE LAMB: An Easter Bible Study** *[Published © 2014; 280 pages; paperback (also available in hardcover)]* Contrary to popular (secular) opinion, I believe the most important season of the Christian calendar is not Christmas, but Easter.  While it is wonderful to enjoy the festivities surrounding the birth of Jesus Christ, there is so much more richness and significance in the last days of His ministry, and the importance of His death and resurrection yet much of this joy is overlooked.

Many Christians shiver at the horrible details of Christ's unjust arrest, His brutal beatings, the farcical trials, that humiliating trudge to Golgotha, and finally, His gruesome death. Subsequently, they hesitate to discuss these facts with their children, or even among themselves. Then comes the substitution of twinkly-nosed bunnies, fluffy chicks, curly-coated lambs, colorful eggs, and all kinds of foil-wrapped chocolates seemingly benign "thieves" taking unlawful precedence over the real story.  *Behold the Lamb* is a fresh, enlightening, entertaining, even provocative study on the Season of the Lamb.

**E-JEANNE:  2003** *[Published © 2013; 680 pages; paperback]* Once upon a time (okay, early in 2000), I began assembling my random musings (later known as "e-Editorials"), cutting-and-pasting articles that interested me, compiling jokes I thought were funny, and then almost on a daily basis  joyfully spamming my family and friends through e-mail.  This precursor to now-popular blogs was modestly called *e-Jeanne* ....

**E-JEANNE:  2004 (Part One - January through June)** *[Published © 2013; 464 pages; paperback]* "Once I got started, I couldn't stop."  The history of *e-Jeanne* began around 1999, really ramped up when 9/11 hit our nation, became more organized

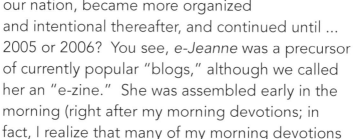

and intentional thereafter, and continued until ... 2005 or 2006?  You see, *e-Jeanne* was a precursor of currently popular "blogs," although we called her an "e-zine."  She was assembled early in the morning (right after my morning devotions; in fact, I realize that many of my morning devotions somehow crept into the e-Editorials), and then forwarded by e-mail to over 300 people all around the world. I did this two or three days a week for 10 years. Like I said, maybe I am a little crazy. ...

This is not a book you can rush through (unless you are only looking for the jokes), and I am astonished how small the font has to be in order to fit everything in; you're going to need a bookmark to help mark your spot. Always, my goal was to fulfill: *"Let your good works shine out for all to see, so that everyone will praise your Heavenly Father."* (Matthew 5:16)

**E-JEANNE: 2004 (Part Two - July through December)**
*[Published © 2013; 484 pages; paperback]* e-Jeanne was a precursor of currently popular "blogs," although we called her an "e-zine." She was assembled early in the morning (right after my morning devotions; in fact, I realize that many of my morning devotions somehow crept into the e-Editorials), and then forwarded by e-mail to over 300 people all around the world. I did this two or three days a week for 10 years. Like I said, maybe I am a little crazy. ...

2004 was a lengthy year, filled with commentary about the impending American Presidential Election (yes, George W. Bush won again), fluctuating health issues, and much sharing of prayer requests and praise reports among the faithful and beloved Readers. 2004 was so lengthy that I had to split it into two books; this is Part Two, covering July through December. Like its sister books, *e-Jeanne: 2004 (Part Two)* comes out looking like a fair-sized phone book; you'll need strong arms and strong hands to hold it while reading ... and I strongly suggest you have a sturdy bookmark.

**E-JEANNE: Remnants (2002, 2005, 2006)** *[Published © 2013; 232 pages; paperback]* The final installment in the *"e-Jeanne"* series [including *e-Jeanne: 2003, e-Jeanne: 2004 (January through June, e-Jeanne: 2004 (July through December)]*, *"e-Jeanne Remnants: 2002, 2005, 2008"* is the adventure of an ordinary North American woman as she lived through a watershed decade. Packed with humor, confrontation, wisdom, silliness, life and death, health and illness - all the normal components of life), Jeanne Halsey's "online journals" made for in-depth and interesting reading. *"A must-read for* *anyone interested in real life in North America as told by an honest writer."* ~ Gloria Edwards

**JUDY BECOMES A BRIDE**
*[Published © 2013; 140 pages; paperback]* 18 days. That's all we had from that first night when we heard the prognosis of the surgeon: *"It's cancer. All throughout her abdomen."* After more tests, we were told "3 to 6 months, if we're lucky." But Judy Gossett was not "lucky" this time and we had 18 days with her before she breathed her last on December 11, 2003. While the shock and heavy sorrow have faded somewhat in these past 10 years, there still remains a surreal nature to life because Judy  she of the huge personality, the enormous heart, the generous spirit, the wonderful sister who was only one year my senior is gone from this life forever. In addition to serving as a tribute to Judy, I pray this book will help people who deal with the grief of losing a beloved person  a sister, a brother, a father, a mother, a wife, a husband, a child, a friend – and understand that the Body of Jesus Christ is often *"the fellowship of suffering"* and is a safe place to find comfort and understanding, to find purpose and meaning.

## THE LEGACY OF WRITING

*[Second Edition; published © 2013; 188 pages; paperback]* An experienced, published writer teaches a Creative Christian Writing Class, using humor, anecdotes and simple facts.

## THE PARABLE OF AURELIA

*[Published © 2012; 112 pages; paperback]* People wonder why Life is so difficult, why it seems we lose more than we gain ... when despite our best efforts we are continually diminished by hurts, disappointments, shattered dreams.  This parable for the 21st century offers an understanding of why and how God is shaping us for greater purposes than we can even dream!

**SHAME-FREE**  *[Published © 2010; 88 pages; paperback]* How parents can survive their teenager's crisis pregnancy.

## STUBBORN FAITH:  Celebrating Joyce Gossett

*[Published © 2011; 162 pages; paperback]* As we commemorate the 20th year of my mother Joyce

Gossett's Home-going, I want to honor her memory and the incredible legacy she left for me and our entire family. I choose to not forget this remarkable woman of God who changed the world because of her stubborn faith in Jesus Christ.

**THREE STRIKES: Dealing With the Sins of Apathy, Unbelief and Ingratitude** *[Published © 2011; 124 pages; paperback]* Apathy, unbelief and ingratitude are three attitudes threatening the Christian Church and undermining the lives of Christians. This book addresses those three sins and offers Bible answers to overturn these failings and walk fresh and strong in Jesus Christ!

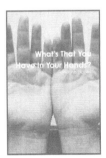

**WHAT'S THAT YOU HAVE IN YOUR HANDS?** *[Published © 2010; 128 pages; paperback]* Fresh air and hope for the weary soul

## Fiction

**A BIBLE FANTASY FOR JUDE, AVA, AJA, AND HAYLEY** *[Published © 2012; 114 pages; full-*

*color, paperback]* Four modern-day children are magically transported back to Bible days, where they meet - and play with - Jesus Christ in the middle of the Sea of Galilee ... then hear Him teach the "Sermon on the Mount" ... then share their lunch with Him as He "feeds the 5,000." All from the imagination of gifted writer Jeanne Halsey, and partially illustrated by two of her three granddaughters ... who also star in the story!

**A CHRISTMAS FANTASY FOR JUDE AND AVA** *[Published © 2011; 112 pages; full-color, paperback]* Jeanne "Grammy" Halsey loves to tell stories to her grandchildren ... and *about* her grandchildren! This 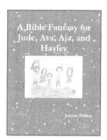 fantasy where Jude and Ava magically travel back in time ... meet a mysterious, sweet lady ... and experience the Birth of Jesus Christ is a tribute to great-Aunty Judy Gossett, who left this Earth before either her great-nephew or great-niece were even born.

**AND GOD CREATED THEATRE** *[Published © 2011; 242 pages; paperback]* Just as Music and Dance have become commonly

accepted forms of Worship in today's Christian church, I believe it is time to rediscover and reclaim the rightful role of Theatre.

**ANOTHER CHANCE: A One-Act Easter Play** *[Published © 2011; 116 pages; paperback]* How did Simon Peter genuinely feel during the difficult hours between the arrest, trial, death, and then the resurrection of Jesus Christ? Not yet knowing that Jesus was alive once more, how could he – or anyone – ever expect to have another chance?

**ANOTHER CHRISTMAS FANTASY FOR JUDE, AVA AND AJA**
*[Published © 2011; 84 pages; full-color, paperback]* In this sequel to *"A Christmas Fantasy for Jude and Ava,"* popular writer Jeanne Halsey adds another grandchild to join in an imaginative adventure back to the time of the birth of Jesus Christ, again aided by a mysterious lady who turns out to be their great-aunt Judy Gossett, who died before any of them were born.

**MESSIAH! BRIGHT MORNING STAR: The Stage Play** *[Published © 2011; 96 pages; paperback]* The Three Wise Guys (also known as "the Three

Wise Men") bumble across to Bethlehem ... Joseph displays new-father jitters ... and Angels eagerly watch from Heaven to see how it all turns out. *"Messiah! Bright Morning Star: The Stage Play"* is a collaboration between noted playwright Jeanne Halsey and award-winning songwriters Reba Rambo and Dony McGuire; a wonderful, humorous musical play!

## NOAH'S ARK: Another Bible Fantasy With Jude, Ava, Aja, Hayley, and Jack and Piper

*[Published © 2014; 84 pages; full-color, paperback]* The greatest art of a Story-Teller is to bring the Reader into the story too, so it often takes "leaps of faith" to reinvent the world as we know it. What child would not like to imagine himself walking up the ramp into Noah's Ark, leading his favorite animals? And what child would not like to look up into the sky when Noah pointed at the rainbow which God had set as a promise, and say in her heart, "That is God's promise for me too"? And what child would not like to pretend to water-ski behind the world's first ocean-liner?

*All titles can be purchased directly from www.Lulu.com or from www.Amazon.com*

## Ghostwriting
*Books Jeanne has written for other authors*

- **BREAK THE GENERATION CURSE** for **Marilyn Hickey**
- *The CARPATHIAN GAMBIT* for **Pastor Steve Watt**
- **FOREVER AND EVER, AMEN** for **Paul Overstreet**
- *GOD 101* for **Pastor Kurt Langstraat**
- *GOD'S ELIXIR FOR LIFE: Psalm 23* for **Pastor Bob Marvel**
- **GREAT TRANSACTIONS OF THE POWER OF GOD** for **Rev. William C. Shackelford**
- **IF NOBODY REACHES, NOBODY GETS TOUCHED** for **Dr. Don Gossett**
- *IMPACT ANALYSIS: A Layman's Journey Through the Evidence* for **Brandon Gossett**
- **LEADING WORSHIP** for **Mark Cole**
- **LIVING ON THE EDGE** for **Sarah Bowling**
- **MARK MY WORDS** for **Rev. Reinhard Bonnke**
- **SOLUTIONS** for **Sarah Bowling**
- *SOWING THE SEEDS OF GOD: Avoiding Compassion Burnout* for **Pastor Steve Scroggins**
- **SUMMIT DANCER** for **Reba Rambo-McGuire**
- *365 DAYS* for **Pastor Frank Colacurcio**

- ***UNLIMITED POTENTIAL IN CHRIST*** for **Dr. Kim O. Ryan**

## Postscript: MY FATHER'S SMILE

People have been asking me what I miss the most about my father. They realize our mourning family is now in that inevitable time of transition where we are experiencing the "firsts": we've already had our first Christmas without Dad, and didn't get to hear him sing his customary jazz version of *"Silent Night"* ... we've had our first Super Bowl Party without Dad (*"Sorry, Seattle Seahawks, you were robbed"*) ... we've already had a handful of family birthday celebrations without Dad sitting at his customary place at the table ... and soon we'll reach the day when there will **not** be – for the first time in over 50 years – Dad's *Annual Good Friday Rally* "at High Noon" in downtown Vancouver. Having already gone through the stages of grief when both my mother and then my sister left the family, at least I know some of what to expect.

Yes, I will miss picking up Dad and driving him to his physiotherapy appointments, helping him in and out of the car and wrangling with his walker. Yes, I will miss sitting next to him in his "alcove" upstairs at his house, and fervently talking about our mutual love of writing. Yes, I will miss our telephone calls, and how he was always so quick and spontaneous to take all matters to prayer.

But I think that, most of all, I am going to miss my father's smile.

You'll be hard-pressed to find a photo of him where he isn't smiling, teeth sparkling, eyes shining. From childhood I remember that my father was always a cheerful, upbeat, warm-hearted man who was quick to smile, and slow to frown or be unhappy. Many people have told me they never heard him say an unkind word about anyone or anything. It wasn't that Dad didn't have sadness or sorrow, or pain or anxiety, or setbacks or disappointments in his life ... but Dad did have a secret: **my father's heart was constantly filled with the joy of the Lord.**

Dad wrote a series of *"Power Poems,"* and – surprise! – they all had Bible verses to underscore them; here are just a few:

- **"A smile is my style"** – *"Rejoice, because your names are written down in Heaven."* (Luke 10:20)
- **"There is no room for gloom"** – *"Serve the LORD with gladness."* (Psalm 100:2)
- **"Fear has no part in my heart"** – *"God has not given me the spirit of fear."* (2 Timothy 1:7)
- **"Good cheer is now here"** – *"In the world you will have tribulation, but be of good cheer for I have overcome the world."* (John 16:33)

- ***"I rejoice in Christ my choice"*** *– "Rejoice in the Lord always, and again I say, rejoice."* (Philippians 4:4)
- ***"I live to give"*** *– "It is more blessed to give than to receive."* (Acts 20:32)
- ***"I practice the attitude of gratitude"*** *– "In everything give thanks, for this is the will of God."* (1 Thessalonians 5:18)

Dad was the real deal. He had saturated his heart and mind with the Word of God, and the joy of the Lord flowed through him all the time, in every circumstance, without hesitation or restriction. Being filled with God's Word and God's Spirit caused my father to smile. And now I miss his smile.

My father didn't raise his children to be defeated Christians. I admit I have a problem singing a song in church that says something like, *"I'm so unworthy, miserable and weak"* because I was raised to believe that I am chosen, accepted and filled with the power of God!

*You are of God, little children, and have overcome them because He Who is in you is greater than he who is in the world.*
**1 John 4:4**; NLT

It makes far more sense for me to sing that little chorus (by an unknown author) which Judy taught us at *Vancouver Christian Centre* so many years ago:

> *I am somebody, I am somebody*
> *I've been washed in the Blood*
> *I am filled with His love*
> *In Jesus, I am somebody!*

Along with such unshakable faith in the power of Christ Jesus at work in me comes that desire to smile, to radiate the love of God to others. It's called the *"gift of encouragement"* (see Romans 12:8), and it is based on childhood training by a man who was always smiling.

> *Is there any encouragement from belonging to Christ? Any comfort from His love? Any fellowship together in the Spirit? Are your hearts tender and compassionate? Then make me truly happy by agreeing wholeheartedly with each other, loving one another, and working together with one mind and purpose. Don't be selfish; don't try to impress others. Be humble, thinking of others as better than yourselves. Don't look out only for your own interests, but take an interest in others too. ...*

*Live clean, innocent lives as children of God, shining like bright lights in a world full of crooked and perverse people. Hold firmly to the Word of Life; then, on the day of Christ's return, I will be proud that I did not run the race in vain and that my work was not useless. But I will rejoice even if I lose my life, pouring it out like a liquid offering to God, just like your faithful service is an offering to God. And I want all of you to share that joy! Yes, you should rejoice, and I will share your joy.*

**Philippians 2:1-4, 15b-18;** NLT

Let me close this book by offering you a challenge: **smile!** Remember Don Gossett, and smile often and always. You too will make the world a better place.